Collins

KS2 Grammar, Punctuation & Spelling

Study & Practice Book

Shelley Welsh

How to use this book

This Grammar, Punctuation and Spelling Study and Practice book contains all the grammar, punctuation and spelling topics children need for key stage 2 in one book.

A **study page** and a **practice page** for each topic.

Tips give ideas on how to remember key information.

'Remember' boxes highlight key points

Key words highlighted on each Study page with definitions in the glossary.

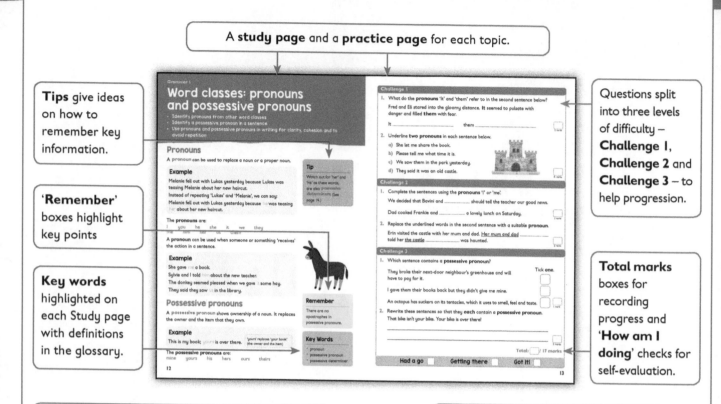

Questions split into three levels of difficulty – **Challenge 1**, **Challenge 2** and **Challenge 3** – to help progression.

Total marks boxes for recording progress and **'How am I doing'** checks for self-evaluation.

Four **Progress tests** included throughout the book for ongoing assessment and monitoring progress.

Mixed questions for Grammar, Punctuation and Spelling Study and Practice book from throughout the book.

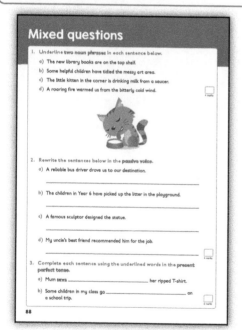

Answers provided for all the questions.

Contents

Word classes: nouns

- Identify nouns from other word classes
- Identify proper nouns and use initial capital letters to spell them

Nouns

Nouns are naming words for people, places, animals and things. These nouns are sometimes called **common nouns**.

Example

boy   dog
tree   school
village   teacher

Collective nouns name a group of things or people.

Example

a herd of cows   a football team   an army of ants
a swarm of bees   a gaggle of geese   a class of pupils

Proper nouns can name a *particular* person or place. They start with a capital letter.

The days of the week, months of the year, titles (for books, plays and films) and planets are also **proper nouns**.

Example

Mr Smith   Sami   Manchester   Chiverton Primary School
Australia   Buckingham Palace   Friday   May
A Boy Called Hope   Romeo and Juliet
Star Wars   Venus

Abstract nouns name feelings, experiences or ideas that you cannot see or touch.

Example

love   hate   satisfaction
courage   friendship   loyalty

Remember

Proper nouns *always* start with a capital letter.

Tip

To help you identify an abstract noun, ask yourself if you can modify it with a determiner such as 'a', 'the', 'my' or 'some'. E.g. I showed **my love** for Gran by buying her a bunch of flowers. There was **some satisfaction** in knowing our rivals had lost the league.

Remember

A determiner is a word such as 'the', 'a' and 'an' that can be used for a specific (known) noun, or a non-specific (unknown) noun. For example, **The** book over there is mine. Maddie gave Gregor **a** book. (See page 14.)

Key Words

- noun
- collective noun
- proper noun
- abstract noun
- determiner

Challenge 1

1. Underline **two nouns** in each sentence below.

   a) He switched his computer on and sat down at his desk.

   b) I hurt my knee during the match.

   c) Black ice can make footpaths very dangerous to walk on.

   d) Penguins have flippers to help them swim.

   4 marks

Challenge 2

1. Which sentence is punctuated correctly?

   Tick **one**.

   In the Summer term, our teacher read us a book called the Hobbit. ☐

   In the Summer term, our Teacher read us a book called the Hobbit. ☐

   In the summer term, our teacher read us a book called The Hobbit. ☐

   1 mark

2. Underline **three nouns** in the sentence below.

   As we listened to the incredible music, we felt the passion of the talented musicians.

   3 marks

Challenge 3

1. Sort the **nouns** below into the correct columns in the table.

   giraffe   disgrace   pleasure   paint   disappointment   screen

   insect   mystery   rage   bubble   mood   feather

Common nouns	Abstract nouns

   12 marks

2. Rewrite the sentence below using correct punctuation.

   Last thursday, we took the bus to nottingham for our weekly Swimming Lesson.

   _____

   _____

   4 marks

   Total: ☐ / 24 marks

   Had a go ☐   **Getting there** ☐   **Got it!** ☐

5

Word classes: adjectives and noun phrases

- Identify adjectives from other word classes
- Use adjectives to make noun phrases

Adjectives

An **adjective** provides more information about a noun, pronoun or proper noun.

Example

Enormous waves surged in the angry ocean as the brave sailors battled to steady the listing boat.

noun modified by an adjective

We were upset to see the awful damage to our lovely garden.

pronoun modified by an adjective

Stefi is usually calm and quiet but today she has been very agitated.

proper noun modified by an adjective

An adjective can **compare** two nouns, pronouns or proper nouns. For adjectives with more than two syllables, insert 'more' or 'most'.

Example

Sam is taller than Aisha.

Cinderella is more beautiful than her step-sisters.

Beth is the most sensible girl in Year 6.

Noun phrases

When you modify a **noun** with another word, e.g. a determiner and/or an adjective, it becomes a **noun phrase**.

Example

our well-stocked library ← determiner adjective noun

Noun phrases can be expanded further. These are called **expanded noun phrases**.

Example

our well-stocked library **full of interesting books**

Remember

Pronouns are 'I', 'you', 'she', 'he', 'it', 'we' and 'they', which replace a noun or a proper noun. (See page 12.)

Tip

A phrase doesn't contain a verb; a **clause** does.

Remember

A noun phrase is a phrase where a noun is the main word, modified by another word or words.

Key Words

- adjective
- noun phrase
- expanded noun phrase
- pronoun

Challenge 1

1. Underline **two adjectives** in each sentence.

   a) The children are going home now after a long, hard day of tests and revision.

   b) Ravi is bored as it hasn't stopped raining and he wants to play football with his best friend.

   c) Dad likes to wear his stripy shirt when he goes to a fancy restaurant with Mum.

   d) The blue whale, weighing approximately 150 tons, is the largest animal on Earth.

4 marks

Challenge 2

1. Underline the **longest noun phrase** in each sentence below.

   a) Thick snow lay on the fields around the farmhouse.

   b) The jubilant crowd cheered as the players received the huge, silver cup adorned with ribbons.

   c) We arrived at the big house and looked at the wooden door with its enormous brass handle.

   d) Our Christmas tree is decorated with a variety of glittery gold and silver baubles.

4 marks

2. Write a sentence of your own containing a **noun phrase**.

   _____

2 marks

Challenge 3

1. Insert the correct form of the **adjective** in brackets to complete each sentence.

   a) Orla is _____ (hungry) than Jack.

   b) Rory's story is _____ (interesting) than mine.

   c) Dan's fancy-dress costume is the _____ (impressive) of them all.

3 marks

2. Add more information to each noun phrase to make an **expanded noun phrase**.

   the mountains _____

   the sky _____

2 marks

Total: ____ / 15 marks

| Had a go ☐ | Getting there ☐ | Got it! ☐ |

7

Word classes: verbs and adverbs

- Identify verbs from other word classes
- Identify adverbs from other word classes
- Use adverbs to modify adjectives and other adverbs

Verbs

A **verb** tells you what someone or something in a sentence is doing, being or having. To identify the verb, find the person or thing in the sentence that is *doing*, *being* or *having*.

Example

Our dog barks at the cat next door.
Amelie is bored today.
My sister has a bad cold and a tickly cough.

> 'Our dog' is 'doing' the action of barking, 'Amelie' is 'being' bored and 'My sister' is 'having' a bad cold.

Adverbs

An **adverb** can modify a verb by saying more about the manner in which something happens. It can also modify an adjective, another adverb or a whole clause.

Example

Ester hungrily ate her breakfast of porridge and banana.

> The adverb modifies the **verb** 'ate' and shows the manner in which Ester ate.

The science test was really difficult today. ← The adverb modifies the **adjective** 'difficult'.

Joe ran very quickly inside to escape the annoying puppy. ← The adverb modifies the **adverb** 'quickly'.

Unfortunately, sports day was cancelled.

> The adverb modifies the **clause** 'sports day was cancelled'.

An adverb can also say *where* something happens, *when* something happens and the *frequency* that something happens.

Example

"Please put your books there," said the teacher.
Come and see me later.
I often go swimming with Markus.

Tip

Some words belong to more than one word class, e.g. 'hard' can be an adjective or an adverb.

Remember

Not all adverbs end in '-ly'.

Key Words

- verb
- adverb

1. Underline **two verbs** in each sentence.

    a) We ran to the shop and ordered vanilla and chocolate ice-creams.

    b) The rain lashes against the window as we stare out of the classroom window.

    c) Bethan usually eats her sandwiches with Bill, but today he is absent.

    d) Mum wants a new car; unfortunately, she hasn't enough money.

    e) My dog, Monty, is a loyal companion who has a calm and friendly temperament.

10 marks

1. Underline the **adverb** in each sentence.

    a) The farmer carefully placed the new-born chicks in the hay.

    b) I'm going home early today as I have a dentist appointment.

    c) Our teacher occasionally lets us go on an early break.

    d) Harry's cousin has never been to a firework display.

4 marks

2. Insert a suitable **adverb** into the sentence below.

    After her run, Ella drank _____ from the water fountain.

1 mark

1. Underline the **adverb** that modifies an adjective in the sentence below.

    J K Rowling's new book is quite good, but I much prefer her last one.

1 mark

2. Underline the **adverb** that modifies another adverb in the sentence below.

    Mum answered the phone rather sleepily as she had slept in.

1 mark

3. Write the word class of the word 'hard' as it is used in each sentence below.

    Today's maths test was very <u>hard</u>.   _____

    Jon worked <u>hard</u> in today's maths test.   _____

2 marks

4. Write a sentence where the word 'fast' is used as an **adverb**.

    _____

2 marks

Total: [   ] / 21 marks

Had a go [ ]   **Getting there** [ ]   **Got it!** [ ]

Word classes: adverbials

- Identify an adverbial in a sentence
- Recognise and use fronted adverbials in writing

Adverbials

An **adverbial** is a word or phrase that is used like an **adverb** to modify a **verb** or **clause**.

Example

Sally and Gus are going to watch a film after dinner.

Alice moved her desk against the wall.

When Dad's new car broke down, he contacted the garage in a foul mood.

> The adverbial phrase 'after dinner' tells the reader when Sally and Gus will watch a film. It modifies the clause 'Sally and Gus are going to watch a film'.

> The adverbial phrase 'against the wall' tells the reader where Alice moved her desk to. It modifies the clause 'Alice moved her desk'.

> The adverbial phrase 'in a foul mood' tells the reader the manner in which Dad contacted the garage. It modifies the verb 'contacted'.

Fronted adverbials

When an adverb or adverbial comes at the beginning of a sentence, it is called a **fronted adverbial**. A fronted adverbial is followed by a **comma**.

Example

Last week, we completed our science investigation.

Some sentences 'work' whether the adverbial is at the end or the beginning of the sentence.

Example

In ten minutes, the bus will arrive.

The bus will arrive in ten minutes.

But look at the difference in meaning between these sentences.

Example

Sadly, Gran's cat Tilly was run over but she's on the mend now.

Gran's cat Tilly was run over but she's on the mend now sadly.

Remember

A fronted adverbial is always followed by a comma.

Key Words

- adverbial
- clause
- fronted adverbial

1. Underline the **adverbial** in each sentence below.

   a) Our school was presented with the football league cup last week.

   b) We have won every year since I've been playing.

   c) As I am the team captain, I politely shook hands with the head teacher.

   d) A photographer took our picture and everyone cheered excitedly.

   4 marks

1. Rewrite each sentence so that it starts with the **adverbial**.

   a) We reached the platform with no time to lose.

   _____

   b) They could see for miles from the top of the summit.

   _____

   c) Gretchen brushed the kitchen floor energetically.

   _____

   d) Fiona was given a new laptop for her special birthday.

   _____

   4 marks

1. Write a sentence starting with a **fronted adverbial** about something you did at the weekend.

   _____

   _____

   2 marks

2. Insert suitable **adverbials** into the passage below. Think about 'where' and 'when' each event could have happened to help you.

   We ate our picnic _____ . _____ ,

   Bella said she wanted to play cricket. The sun blazed _____ ,

   so we set our game up in the shade. It was growing dark when we left

   _____ .

   4 marks

   Total: ____ / 14 marks

| Had a go ☐ | Getting there ☐ | Got it! ☐ |

Word classes: pronouns and possessive pronouns

- Identify pronouns from other word classes
- Identify a possessive pronoun in a sentence
- Use pronouns and possessive pronouns in writing for clarity, cohesion and to avoid repetition

Pronouns

A **pronoun** can be used to replace a noun or a proper noun.

Example

Melanie fell out with Lukas yesterday because Lukas was teasing Melanie about her new haircut.

Instead of repeating 'Lukas' and 'Melanie', we can say:

Melanie fell out with Lukas yesterday because he was teasing her about her new haircut.

The **pronouns** are:

I	you	he	she	it	we	they
me	him	her	us	them		

A **pronoun** can be used when someone or something 'receives' the action in a sentence.

Example

She gave me a book.

Sylvie and I told him about the new teacher.

The donkey seemed pleased when we gave it some hay.

They said they saw us in the library.

Possessive pronouns

A **possessive pronoun** shows ownership of a noun. It replaces the owner and the item that they own.

Example

This is my book; yours is over there.

> 'yours' replaces 'your book' (the owner and the item)

The **possessive pronouns** are:

mine   yours   his   hers   ours   theirs

> **Tip**
>
> Watch out for 'her' and 'his' as these words, are also **possessive determiners**. (See page 14.)

> **Remember**
>
> There are no apostrophes in possessive pronouns.

> **Key Words**
>
> - pronoun
> - possessive pronoun
> - possessive determiner

Challenge 1

1. What do the **pronouns** 'It' and 'them' refer to in the second sentence below?

   Fred and Eli stared into the gloomy distance. **It** seemed to pulsate with danger and filled **them** with fear.

   It _____   them _____

   2 marks

2. Underline **two pronouns** in each sentence below.

   a) She let me share the book.

   b) Please tell me what time it is.

   c) We saw them in the park yesterday.

   d) They said it was an old castle.

   8 marks

Challenge 2

1. Complete the sentences using the **pronouns** 'I' or 'me'.

   We decided that Bavini and _____ should tell the teacher our good news.

   Dad cooked Frankie and _____ a lovely lunch on Saturday.

   2 marks

2. Replace the underlined words in the second sentence with a suitable **pronoun**.

   Erin visited the castle with her mum and dad. <u>Her mum and dad</u> _____ told her <u>the castle</u> _____ was haunted.

   2 marks

Challenge 3

1. Which sentence contains a **possessive pronoun**?

   Tick **one**.

   They broke their next-door neighbour's greenhouse and will have to pay for it. ☐

   I gave them their books back but they didn't give me mine. ☐

   An octopus has suckers on its tentacles, which it uses to smell, feel and taste. ☐

   1 mark

2. Rewrite these sentences so that they **each** contain a **possessive pronoun**.
   That bike isn't your bike. Your bike is over there!

   _____

   _____

   2 marks

   Total: ☐ / 17 marks

Had a go ☐   **Getting there** ☐   **Got it!** ☐

13

Word classes: determiners and possessive determiners

- Identify determiners from other word classes
- Use appropriate determiners in your writing

Determiners

A **determiner** is a word that introduces a **noun**. It tells us whether the noun is specific (known) or non-specific (unknown).

Example

Anya gave me the book about sea creatures that I wanted.

> The book is specific or known.

Anya gave me a book about sea creatures.

> The book is non-specific or unknown.

The determiner comes before any modifiers that come before the noun.

Example

I ventured further into the murky, deep depths of the forest.

determiner   adjectives   noun

The **determiner a** becomes **an** if it is used before a vowel.

Example

An ant was crawling on an enormous apple.

Other **determiners** include:

this, that, these, those, some, every, none, lots of, one, two, three

Possessive determiners

A **possessive determiner** shows ownership of the noun that follows it.

Example

Maya said her naughty dog had eaten its collar so she couldn't walk with me and my dog.

> **Tip**
>
> To find the determiner in a sentence, find the noun. Though bear in mind, an adjective might come in between.

> **Remember**
>
> Never use an apostrophe in the possessive determiner 'its'; 'it's' always means 'it is'.

> **Key Words**
>
> - determiner
> - possessive determiner

Challenge 1

1. Underline **three determiners** in each sentence below.

   a) After Dad found a film we all wanted to watch on the TV, he handed out some chocolate brownies.

   b) Those children have been accused of dropping lots of litter in the playground.

   c) Two field mice appeared in the farmer's kitchen after the wheat was harvested.

   d) Each apple we took from the tree was crunchy, crisp and cool, and we savoured every bite.

   12 marks

Challenge 2

1. Insert suitable **possessive determiners** in the sentences below.

   a) Harry did _____ homework, then packed _____ schoolbag ready for the morning.

   b) _____ teacher is leaving to travel the world with _____ husband.

   c) Ella said _____ dog had been missing since she came back from _____ piano lesson.

   d) I think _____ handwriting has improved since I've started holding _____ pencil differently.

   8 marks

Challenge 3

1. Insert suitable **determiners** in the passage below. Try not to repeat any!

   _____ children eat _____ fruit. Personally, I eat _____

   portions _____ day. I also like to do _____ exercise on

   _____ daily basis. There is _____ doubt that I feel and look

   healthier after _____ months of following _____ routine.

   9 marks

Total: ☐ / 29 marks

Had a go ☐   **Getting there** ☐   **Got it!** ☐

15

Word classes: prepositions

- Identify prepositions from other word classes
- Use appropriate prepositions in your writing

Prepositions

A **preposition** shows the relationship between a **noun**, **proper noun** or **pronoun** and other words in a sentence or clause. Common prepositions include: at, by, for, from, in, of, on, to, with

A preposition can show position or location.

Example

My book is on the table. Your pen is under your chair.
Someone is at the door.

A preposition can show direction.

Example

We drove towards the farm. Kay dived into the sea.
Dougie sent a card to his cousin.

A preposition can show time.

Example

Meet me at one o'clock. I'm staying for two days.
Dad will be home in an hour.

A preposition can also introduce an **object**. The object in a sentence is what the **subject** is 'acting upon'. (See page 18.)

Example

I like a piece of toast for breakfast.

Some prepositions are used to introduce the object of a verb.

Example

She glanced at the strange man.
Bill looked for his keys.
He didn't approve of her behaviour.

Remember

Some words, such as the prepositions 'after' and 'before', belong to more than one word class.

Key Words

- preposition
- object

1. Underline **two prepositions** in each sentence below.

   a) Valerie took the bus into town and met Juliette at the shops.

   b) I put my dish of ice-cream on the table.

   c) Freddie goes to his swimming lesson at 3 o'clock.

   d) The children walked across the bridge and sat beside the river.

   8 marks

1. Use a minimum of **four prepositions** to write a set of instructions on how to get from your front door to your bedroom, or from your house to your school.

   _____

   _____

   _____

   _____

   4 marks

2. Complete the sentences below with suitable prepositions.

   Anya sat _____ me _____ the bus when we

   went _____ our school trip _____ the Lake

   District. We arrived _____ 11 o'clock and had our lunch

   _____ some picnic tables _____ the river.

   7 marks

1. Draw a line to match each verb to the **preposition** that it takes. Use a dictionary to help you.

approve	for	consist	to
stare	of	lend	with
hope	in	blame	on
believe	to	borrow	of
dedicate	at	compare	from

   10 marks

   Total: [ ] / 29 marks

| **Had a go** [ ] | **Getting there** [ ] | **Got it!** [ ] |

Subject and object

- Identify the subject in a sentence
- Identify the object in a sentence
- Understand that the subject must 'agree' with the verb

The subject

The **subject** of a sentence is the person or thing that is carrying out the action, shown by the **verb**. The verb tells you what the subject is 'doing', 'being' or 'having'. The subject can be a **noun**, **proper noun**, **pronoun** or **noun phrase**.

Tip

To help you find the subject in a sentence, find the verb and see who or what is 'doing', 'being' or 'having'.

Example

People often go to the seaside in summer. | subject | verb |

Grace and her family are vegetarian. | subject | verb |

We have a new carpet in our living room. | subject | verb |

Mo's elderly great-aunt walks with a stick. | subject | verb |

If the subject is singular, the verb must be in the singular form so that it 'agrees' with the subject.

Example

| singular subject |

Thomas does his homework every night.

| singular verb form |

| plural subject |

We are watching our sister in a play.

| plural verb form |

The object

The **object** of a sentence is the noun, proper noun, pronoun or noun phrase that is being 'acted upon' by the **subject**.

Remember

Not every subject has an object. For example, 'The train arrived punctually.'

Example

Cats like to chase mice. | subject | verb | object |

She has freckles on her cheeks. | subject | verb | object |

Kassim is eating fish, chips and peas. | subject | verb | object |

My sister writes to Myra, who lives in Serbia. | subject | verb | object |

Key Words

- subject
- verb
- object

Challenge 1

1. Underline the **subject** in each sentence below.

   a) Brea helps her mum in the kitchen.

   b) She usually clears the table after meals.

   c) Her dad will then wash the dishes.

   d) Then they all sit down to watch TV.

   4 marks

Challenge 2

1. Which sentence below contains an **object**?

   Tick **one**.

   My friend Judy goes swimming every Saturday.

   Flooding is causing damage to homes in this region.

   Maddie and I are happily dancing.

   The cool sea is so wonderfully refreshing!

   1 mark

2. Insert either **is** or **are** so that the verb agrees with the subject in each sentence.

   The number of children arriving late _____ increasing.

   The good news _____ that we can go home early today.

   The ladies' changing rooms _____ closed today.

   3 marks

Challenge 3

1. Use the word pairs in the box to create sentences where one word is the **subject** and the other the **object**. Remember to punctuate your sentences correctly.

   | 1. the choir / songs | 2. some children / litter | 3. Mr Smith / cakes |

   1. _____

   2. _____

   3. _____

   6 marks

   Total: ____ / 14 marks

   Had a go ☐ **Getting there** ☐ **Got it!** ☐

19

Progress test I

1. Underline **two adjectives** in each sentence below.

   a) My new computer is really fast.

   b) After the heavy rainfall, we discovered a small leak in our attic.

   c) Becky felt miserable when she realised she had upset her best friend.

   d) I am impatient to receive a long letter from my cousin in Spain.

   8 marks

2. What is the **word class** of the underlined words in the sentence below?

   Every day, Mr Burns walks along the river with <u>his little black dog</u>.

	Tick **one**.
a noun	☐
an adverbial	☐
a determiner	☐
a noun phrase	☐

   1 mark

3. Underline **three verbs** in each sentence below.

   a) The bakery sells such tasty pies that I decided to have two.

   b) When Ezra woke, he remembered his terrible dream and panicked.

   c) The hotel guests packed, paid their bill and left.

   d) Will wants to learn Spanish but he finds languages difficult.

   12 marks

4. Which sentence contains a **fronted adverbial**?

	Tick **one**.
There is a new boy in our class called Chen.	☐
Chen, who comes from China, doesn't speak much English.	☐
Callum and I have been helping him learn a few words.	☐
Just last week, Chen mastered all his times tables.	☐

   1 mark

5. **What is the word class of the underlined word in the sentence below?**

Millie's <u>headache</u> became worse as the day progressed.

Tick **one**.

an adverb ☐

a noun ☐

a verb ☐

an adjective ☐

1 mark

6. **Label each box with the correct letter to show the word class of each word indicated by an arrow.**

A	B	C	D	E	F
noun	verb	adjective	adverb	determiner	pronoun

Unfortunately, when we reached the summit, it was covered with a dense mist

☐   ☐ ☐   ☐   ☐

which ruined our view.

☐

6 marks

7. **Underline the determiners in each sentence below.**

a) Sophie usually eats a slice of toast for breakfast but today she had some cereal.

b) The soldiers marched towards the barracks, looking forward to a well-deserved rest.

c) Jenni has two younger sisters and an older brother.

d) We took the late train to Scotland and Gran met us on the platform.

8 marks

8. **Write a sentence using the word <u>hike</u> as a verb.**

_____

Write a sentence using the word <u>hike</u> as a noun.

_____

2 marks

9. Use each picture to write a sentence containing at least one expanded noun phrase.

_____   _____

_____   _____

4 marks

10. Replace the words in brackets in the passage below with suitable pronouns.

Maria and Josef walked to the bus stop. (Maria and Josef) _____ were

late yet again and the bus had already left. Unlike (Maria and Josef)

_____, (the bus) _____ was always punctual. (The children)

_____ went back home to tell their mum. (Mum) _____ was

cross but agreed to take (Maria and Josef) _____ to school in her car.

However, (her car) _____ wouldn't start as (Mum) _____ had

left her lights on, which meant (her car) _____ now had a flat battery.

9 marks

11. Complete the sentence by inserting a suitable **adverb**.

Asqa stirred the mixture _____, then put it into the cake tin.

1 mark

12. What is the word class of the underlined word in the sentence below?

We parked our car next to <u>theirs</u>.

Tick **one**.

a determiner ☐   a possessive determiner ☐

a possessive pronoun ☐   an adverbial ☐

1 mark

13. **Rewrite the sentence below so that it starts with the adverbial.**

We were relieved to get on the ferry after a long wait.

_____

2 marks

14. **What is the word class of each underlined word?**

Christian and Flo <u>care</u> deeply about their sick dog.   _____

Christian and Flo take good <u>care</u> of their sick dog.   _____

2 marks

15. **Underline the object in each sentence below.**

a)   Today, we baked cakes in school.

b)   The dog is eating a bone at the bottom of the garden.

c)   I dropped a glass on the kitchen floor.

d)   The ranger rescued the elephant from the trap.

4 marks

16. **Underline three prepositions in the sentence below.**

I intended to sit beside James, but he wouldn't move over.

3 marks

17. **Which underlined word is an adverb?**

Tick **one**.

Mum told me not to sit on the <u>wobbly</u> chair. ☐

The weather has been <u>lovely</u> today. ☐

Xavier has <u>nearly</u> finished his art project. ☐

Jake has red, <u>curly</u> hair and freckles. ☐

1 mark

18. **What is the word class of the underlined word in the sentence below?**

As Maddie and Pippa ran over the finish line, their Dad took a photo of <u>them</u>.

Tick **one**.

a possessive pronoun	☐	a determiner	☐
a pronoun	☐	a preposition	☐

1 mark

Total: ☐ / 67 marks

Functions of sentences: statements and questions

- Identify and use different sentence types
- Use punctuation correctly

Statements

A **statement** is a sentence that tells you something. It starts with a capital letter and ends with a full stop.

Example

Rory is 11 years old.
We go camping every summer.

Questions

A **question** is a sentence that asks something. It starts with a capital letter and ends with a **question mark**.

Example

How old are you?
Where are my shoes?

A **question** can be in the form of a statement followed by a **question tag**.

Example

You're Eddie's sister, aren't you?
It's hot today, isn't it?
You've read that book, haven't you?

> The verb form in the question tag is negative even though we expect the person to whom we are talking to agree with what we are saying.

> **Remember**
>
> There is a comma between the statement and the question tag.

A **question** can *start* with the question tag.

Example

Aren't you Eddie's sister?
Isn't it hot today?
Haven't you read that book?

> **Key Words**
>
> - statement
> - question
> - question tag

Challenge 1

1. Add the missing final punctuation to each sentence below.

   a) It's time to go home

   c) Are you coming with me

   b) Whose coat is this

   d) We'll be late for the bus

   4 marks

2. Write a **statement** about yourself.

   _____

   1 mark

Challenge 2

1. Use all the words and phrases in the boxes to write a **statement** on the line below.

   | in the farmer's field | a crowd of people | watching |

   | there | the firework display | was |

   _____

   _____

   _____

   1 mark

2. Rewrite this statement as a **question**. Use only the words given.

   Michael has started revising for his test.

   _____

   1 mark

Challenge 3

1. Write a suitable **question** for each answer.

   Question: _____

   Answer: We're spending a week in Scotland in a caravan.

   Question: _____

   Answer: My all-time favourite is 'Harry Potter and the Philosopher's Stone'.

   2 marks

Total: [   ] / 9 marks

Had a go [   ]   **Getting there** [   ]   **Got it!** [   ]

Functions of sentences: commands and exclamations

- Identify and use different sentence types
- Use punctuation correctly

Commands

A **command** sentence contains a **command verb**. It starts with a capital letter and can end with a full stop or an exclamation mark.

Example

Tell me your name.

Please help me lift this chair!

To turn on the laptop, press this button.

Exclamations

An **exclamation sentence** starts with 'What…', or 'How…', contains a verb, and ends with an exclamation mark.

Example

How lovely it is to see you!

How talented that boy is!

What a pleasant surprise to see you!

What a fabulous holiday!

> **Tip**
>
> A command verb can also be called an imperative.

> **Tip**
>
> A command verb doesn't always come at the start of the sentence.

> **Remember**
>
> An **exclamation sentence** contains a verb; otherwise it wouldn't be a sentence. For example, *How lovely!* is an **exclamation**, but it is **not** an exclamation sentence.

> **Key Words**
>
> - command
> - imperative
> - exclamation sentence

26

Challenge 1

1. Underline the **command verb** in each sentence below.

   a) Please help me tidy up the kitchen.

   b) Bring the dog inside please; it's raining!

   c) Carefully mix the butter, sugar and eggs.

   d) Hurry up please – I don't want to miss the start of the show.

   4 marks

Challenge 2

1. Which sentence below is an **exclamation**?

   Tick **one**.

   How many times have I told you to wipe your feet

   What a dreadful night of wind and rain that was

   How was I to know that it was your birthday last week

   What did you think of the meal last night

   1 mark

2. Add a **command verb** to complete each sentence.

   a) _____ your breakfast quickly!

   b) _____ both ways before you cross the road.

   2 marks

Challenge 3

1. Write a **command sentence** of your own.

   _____

   1 mark

2. Write an **exclamation sentence** of your own.

   _____

   1 mark

3. Which sentence must **not** end with an **exclamation mark**?

   Tick **one**.

   How shocking the news was yesterday

   What a terrible thing to happen

   How many people were affected by the storm

   What a beautiful day it is

   1 mark

   Total: ☐ / 10 marks

Had a go ☐   **Getting there** ☐   **Got it!** ☐

27

Combining words, phrases and clauses: coordinating and subordinating conjunctions

- Identify coordinating and subordinating conjunctions
- Use coordinating conjunctions to link two words, phrases or clauses
- Use subordinating conjunctions to link subordinate clauses to main clauses

Coordinating conjunctions

Words, phrases and clauses can be linked (coordinated) as an equal pair by the **coordinating conjunctions** 'and', 'but' and 'or'.

Example

Ursula doesn't like science or maths.

I like PE and English. ← links two **words** as an equal pair

Cal likes PE but I prefer art. ← links two **clauses** as an equal pair

Subordinating conjunctions and subordinate clauses

A **subordinating conjunction** introduces a **subordinate clause**; a **subordinate clause** is dependent on a **main clause**, otherwise it doesn't make sense.

Example

We were tired <u>because</u> we had been playing sport all afternoon.

| main clause | subordinating conjunction | subordinate clause |

Subordinating conjunctions include:

because   although   after   before   as

If a sentence starts with the subordinate clause, it is followed by a **comma**.

Example

We got a table although we hadn't booked.

Although we hadn't booked, we got a table.

> **Tip**
>
> A main clause makes sense on its own; a subordinate clause doesn't.
> When you take away the subordinate clause, the main clause is left.

> **Remember**
>
> A subordinate clause is introduced by a subordinating conjunction.

> **Key Words**
>
> - coordinating conjunction
> - subordinating conjunction
> - subordinate clause
> - main clause

Challenge 1

1. Join the following sentences to make one sentence, using a suitable **coordinating conjunction**.

   Ushma has a dog. She hasn't got a cat.

   _____

   1 mark

2. Insert suitable **coordinating conjunctions** to complete the sentence below.

   Gran told my brother _____ me that we could either read a book _____ watch a film, _____ then we would have to go to bed.

   3 marks

3. Underline the **subordinating conjunction** in each sentence below.

   Dev played football until it started raining.

   The criminals were soon caught as they had been careless.

   2 marks

Challenge 2

1. Tick a box in each row to show whether the underlined words are a **main clause** or a **subordinate clause**.

Sentence	Main clause	Subordinate clause
After we had been swimming, <u>we went to the new restaurant for a pizza</u>.		
Nick was passionate about football <u>even though he'd never been to a big match</u>.		
<u>We managed to make it to school</u> once the icy roads had been gritted.		
Katie said we should meet in the park <u>before we started our sponsored run</u>.		

4 marks

Challenge 3

1. Add a suitable **main clause** to the subordinate clause below to make a full sentence.

   _____ as the sun began to set.

   1 mark

2. Rewrite the sentence below so that it starts with the **subordinate clause**.

   We are going abseiling at the weekend if the weather stays fine.

   _____

   2 marks

   Total: [ ] / 13 marks

Had a go [ ]   **Getting there** [ ]   **Got it!** [ ]

Combining words, phrases and clauses: relative clauses

- Identify relative pronouns and relative clauses
- Use relative clauses in writing

Relative clauses

A **relative clause** gives more information about the preceding **noun**. It is introduced by a **relative pronoun**.

Relative pronouns

The relative pronouns are:

who   which   that   whose   where   when

- 'who' is used for people or pets
- 'which' is used for things
- 'that' can be used for people or things
- 'whose' is used to show that the following noun belongs to the preceding noun, noun phrase or proper noun.

Example

That book <u>that</u> I was given is a best-seller.

> 'that' refers back to 'That book'

Rachel, <u>who</u> is ten, is having a party.

> 'who' refers back to 'Rachel'

My birthday, <u>when</u> all my family visit, is the best day.

> 'when' refers back to 'My birthday'

The farmer, <u>whose</u> sheep had escaped, was not happy.

> 'whose' refers back to 'The farmer' who owns the sheep

The **relative pronoun** can refer back to the **whole clause**.

Example

Ben baked biscuits, <u>which</u> pleased Carla.

Sometimes, the **relative pronoun** 'that' can be left out.

Example

The horse (<u>that</u>) I rode yesterday is very calm.

Tip

A relative clause is a type of subordinate clause; it doesn't make sense without the main clause.

Remember

A relative clause gives more information about the noun, noun phrase or proper noun which comes before it.

Key Words

- relative clause
- relative pronoun

Challenge 1

1. Underline the **relative clause** in each sentence below.

   a) My cousin, who lives in Scotland, is coming for Christmas.

   b) My great-grandfather was born in 1939, when World War II started.

   2 marks

Challenge 2

1. Insert a suitable **relative pronoun** in each sentence below.

   a) The weather, _____ has been rather grim, has thankfully perked up.

   b) The day _____ my baby brother was born was the best day ever!

   c) Muir's best friend, _____ is moving house, is planning a party.

   d) The shop on the corner, _____ the traffic lights are, is new.

   4 marks

Challenge 3

1. Rewrite the sentences below, so that they do **not** contain a **relative pronoun.**

   The toothache that I had last night has finally eased.

   _____

   _____

   The year when we won the World Cup was amazing!

   _____

   _____

   2 marks

2. In which sentence below could you leave out the **relative pronoun?**

   Tick **one.**

   We've been watching a new TV programme, which has a very complicated plot. ☐

   The cat, whose owner was away, stayed at a neighbour's house. ☐

   The book that I read last year has been made into a film. ☐

   The new boy, who joined our class yesterday, is very shy. ☐

   1 mark

Total: ☐ / 9 marks

Had a go ☐   **Getting there** ☐   **Got it!** ☐

Verb forms and tense: simple present and simple past tenses

- Identify the simple present and simple past tenses
- Use the simple present and simple past tenses

Verbs

Every sentence contains a **verb**, which tells us what the subject is doing, being or having.

Simple present tense

We use verbs in the **simple present tense** to talk about an event or state of being that is happening now or happens regularly.

Example

I feel tired; are you tired?

Dad always tells us when it is time for bed.

Simple past tense

The **simple past tense** is used to talk about an event or state of being or having that has already happened (it is in the past).

Example

Florence looked at her watch.

Jack was hungry.

Were you late again?

We had no time to spare.

You might use a mixture of simple present and simple past tense in your writing, for example, when writing in your diary.

Example

○ **Saturday**
○ Woke up late this morning. It was a cold, miserable
○ day. We went to the park but I slipped in the mud!
○ Came home, had a shower and now I'm ready for
○ something to eat. It's warm and cosy in my bedroom.

> **Remember**
>
> If the subject is singular, the verb must be in the singular form so that it 'agrees' with the subject. For example, She likes ice-cream. They like ice-cream.

> **Remember**
>
> In the simple present tense and the simple past tense, there is only one verb – it's simple! Other tenses have more than one verb part.

> **Key Words**
>
> - simple present tense
> - simple past tense

Challenge 1

1. Change the verbs in bold from the simple present tense to the **simple past tense.**

   Everyone in our class **likes** _____ our new teacher, Mrs Semple.

   She always **helps** _____ and **encourages** _____ us.

   Her motto **is** _____ 'dare to dream!'

   4 marks

Challenge 2

1. Which sentence uses **tense** correctly?

   Tick **one.**

   The doctor assisted the injured player when she limps off the pitch. ☐

   The doctor assist the injured player when she limped off the pitch. ☐

   The doctor assists the injured player when she limped off the pitch. ☐

   The doctor assisted the injured player when she limped off the pitch. ☐

   1 mark

2. Complete each sentence with a suitable verb in the correct **tense.**

   a) This year, we are going to London to stay with our cousins but last year they _____ to us.

   b) Mum is always telling us not to leave lights on but she often _____ to switch them off herself!

   2 marks

Challenge 3

1. Complete each sentence in the **simple past tense** using the verbs in the brackets.

   Mollie _____ (take) great care when she _____ (draw) the map.

   Sol _____ (run) over the finish line and _____ (throw) himself on the ground in relief.

   4 marks

2. Write the **simple past tense** of each verb below.

   catch _____   do _____   drive _____

   buy _____   fight _____   fly _____

   6 marks

   Total: ☐ / 17 marks

Had a go ☐   **Getting there** ☐   **Got it!** ☐

Verb forms and tense: perfect form

- Identify the present perfect and past perfect tenses
- Use the present perfect and past perfect tenses

Present perfect tense

The **present perfect tense** can be used to show an action or state that has been completed at some time in the past.

It is formed by using the **present tense** of 'to have' and the **past participle** of the **verb**.

Example

I think we have met before. ◄── present tense of 'have' (plural) and past participle of 'meet'

The shop has closed for good. ◄── present tense of 'have' (singular) and past participle of 'close'

The present perfect tense can also show an action or state that began in the past and continues to the present time.

Example

The rain has increased in the last hour.

We have had this wet weather since Monday.

Past perfect tense

The **past perfect tense** can be used to show an action that was completed *before* another point in the past.

It is formed by using the **past tense** of the verb 'to have' and the **past participle** of the **verb**.

Example

Just as I had finished my book, Amerjit knocked on the door. ◄── past tense of 'have' and past participle of 'finish'

The shop had closed early. ◄── past tense of 'had' and past participle of 'close'

> **Tip**
>
> The past participle of most verbs is formed by adding '-ed' to the root word. For example, jump**ed**, climb**ed**, cook**ed**.

> **Remember**
>
> Some verbs have an irregular past participle. For example, gone, said, done, thought, eaten.

> **Key Words**
>
> - present perfect tense
> - past participle
> - past perfect tense

Challenge 1

1. Underline the verbs that are in the **present perfect tense**.

   a) Michael has made the decision to train for the London Marathon.

   b) There is a lot of snow so Mum and Dad have decided to take us sledging.

   2 marks

2. Underline the verbs that are in the **past perfect tense**.

   a) Georgie had written a diary regularly for years, then suddenly she stopped.

   b) Nikolas went to the dentist as he had suffered with toothache for weeks.

   2 marks

Challenge 2

1. Write the underlined words in the **present perfect tense**.

   a) Dad <u>took</u> _____ the ferry to France to see his cousin.

   b) I <u>ate</u> _____ a large portion of fish and chips.

   c) Farida <u>does</u> _____ a lot of fundraising for charity.

   d) We <u>are</u> _____ on holiday in Cornwall.

   4 marks

Challenge 3

1. What is the meaning of the sentence below?

   Our neighbours have had chickens for about three years.

   Tick **one**.

   Our neighbours used to have chickens. ☐

   Our neighbours intend to get chickens. ☐

   Our neighbours still have chickens now. ☐

   1 mark

2. Tick the sentence that is in the **past perfect tense**.

   Tick **one**.

   Our class has been learning about the Tudors. ☐

   Mum told me she studied Henry VIII at school. ☐

   She hadn't realised that Henry VIII was so overweight! ☐

   Luckily, that's not the only fact I have remembered. ☐

   1 mark

   Total: ☐ / 10 marks

Had a go ☐   Getting there ☐   Got it! ☐

Verb forms and tense: present and past progressive

- Identify the present progressive and past progressive tenses
- Use the present progressive and past progressive tenses

Present progressive tense

The **present progressive tense** shows an action that is continuing to happen. It is formed from the **simple present tense** of the verb 'to be' and the **present participle** of the **main verb**.

Example

The children are enjoying their summer holidays.

> present tense of 'to be' (plural) and present participle of 'to enjoy'

The fisherman is repairing his net.

> present tense of 'to be' (singular) and present participle of 'to repair'

The present participle is formed by adding the suffix '-ing' to the verb root. For example, run → running.

Past progressive tense

The **past progressive tense** shows a continuous action in the past. It is formed from the **simple past tense** of the verb 'to be' and the **present participle** of the **main verb**.

Example

The waves were crashing on the rocks.

> past tense of 'to be' (plural) and present participle of 'to crash'

Monty was chasing next door's cat.

> past tense of 'to be' (singular) and present participle of 'to chase'

Tip

The present progressive tense can also be used when talking about a future event. For example, 'Bethan **is coming** for a sleepover this weekend'.

Remember

Spelling rules apply! For example:
believe → believing;
swim → swimming

Remember

The **subject** of the sentence must 'agree' with the verb. For example, 'They are running for the last bus.'. The plural pronoun 'They' agrees with the plural verb form 'are'.

Key Words

- present progressive tense
- simple present tense
- present participle
- past progressive tense
- simple past tense

Challenge 1

1. Underline the verbs in the **present progressive tense** in the sentences below.

   a) I'm planning my writing homework using a colour-coded mind map.

   b) We have been thinking about moving to the coast but now Dad is considering other options.

   c) You won't believe who is moving to our neighbourhood next month!

   3 marks

2. Underline the verbs in the **past progressive tense** in the sentences below.

   a) I thought I heard a loud bang but maybe I was dreaming.

   b) As Mum was painting the kitchen, she noticed a damp patch had appeared on the ceiling.

   c) Our uncles were expecting compensation after a car accident in which they broke their arms.

   3 marks

Challenge 2

1. Tick a box to show the tense used in each sentence.

Sentence	Present perfect	Past perfect	Present progressive	Past progressive
Kasim is riding his bike to school this term.				
I had thought he might prefer the bus.				
He has tried cycling in the past.				
However, he was finding it hard in the winter.				

4 marks

Challenge 3

1. Change the underlined verbs so that they are in the **past progressive tense**.

   As Juan <u>walked</u> _____ to the leisure centre, he met Sonia.

   They <u>chatted</u> _____ for a while before they parted company.

   When Juan arrived, the fire alarm <u>rang</u> _____.

   3 marks

Total: ___ / 13 marks

Had a go ☐   **Getting there** ☐   **Got it!** ☐

37

Verb forms and tense: active and passive voice

- Identify the active and passive voice
- Change a sentence from the active to the passive voice and vice versa

Active voice

Mostly, we write and speak in the **active voice**. This means that the **subject** of the sentence is 'doing', 'being' or 'having'. If there is an **object**, the subject is 'acting upon' it.

Tip

The passive voice can be used to convey formality in speech or writing.

Example

Many people watch football matches.

| subject | verb | object |

Passive voice

In the **passive voice**, the noun, noun phrase or pronoun that would have been the **object** in the active voice becomes the **subject**, and 'receives' the action.

The **subject** from the **active voice** sentence does not become the **object**; it becomes part of a **prepositional phrase**.

The **passive voice** is formed by combining the verb 'to be' with the **past participle** of the **verb**.

Example

Football matches are watched by many people.

| noun phrase | present tense of 'to be' and past participle of 'to watch' | prepositional phrase |

Sometimes, the prepositional phrase can be left out.

Example

The winner was announced by the judge.
The winner was announced.

The ball was thrown in the lake by the little girl.
The ball was thrown in the lake.

Key Words

- active voice
- passive voice
- prepositional phrase
- past participle

Challenge 1

1. Tick one box in each row to show whether each sentence is in the **active voice** or the **passive voice**.

Sentence	Active voice	Passive voice
Connie was standing by the door when she heard the bell ring.		
Our dog was treated by the vet when he had kennel cough.		
Harry was announced the winner by the competition judge.		
Mum's temperamental car is usually repaired by Greg, a mechanic.		

4 marks

Challenge 2

1. Underline the subject and circle the object in each **active voice** sentence.

    a) The anglers caught 35kg of fish over the course of the day.

    b) My dog chased your cat into the park.

4 marks

2. Underline the subject and circle the prepositional phrase in each **passive voice** sentence.

    a) My grandad's temperature was taken by a nurse.

    b) We were advised by the police to install an alarm.

4 marks

3. Rewrite each sentence in question 2 above so that they are in the **active voice**.

    a) _____

    b) _____

2 marks

Challenge 3

1. Rewrite the sentence below in the **passive voice**.

    The receptionist checked us in and showed us to our rooms.

    _____

2 marks

2. Rewrite the sentence you have written in the **passive voice** in question 1 above, omitting the prepositional phrase.

    _____

2 marks

Total: [ ] / 18 marks

Had a go [ ]   **Getting there** [ ]   **Got it!** [ ]

39

Verb forms and tense: modal verbs

- Identify modal verbs
- Use modal verbs to express degrees of certainty, ability, permission or obligation
- Use adverbs to express degrees of certainty

Modal verbs

The **modal verbs** are: can could may might must shall should will ought to would

Modal verbs can be used to express degrees of certainty, ability, permission or obligation. They come before the **main verb** in a sentence.

> **Remember**
>
> Both modal verbs and some adverbs can show degrees of certainty.

Example

Expressing degrees of uncertainty:

I may be going swimming this evening. I would offer to take you but there might not be enough room in the car.

Expressing degrees of ability:

Abigail's mum can speak Russian, Czech and French.

Expressing degrees of permission:

"You can go to the park if you tidy your room first," said Dad.

Expressing degrees of obligation:

Tarek said I should offer to help wash the dishes.

Adverbs to express degrees of certainty

Some **adverbs** can also express degrees of certainty.

Example

The dog walker clearly hadn't seen the "Please keep off the grass!" sign. ← Expressing degree of certainty

Perhaps the dog walker hadn't seen the "Please keep off the grass!" sign. ← Expressing degree of uncertainty

> **Key Words**
>
> - modal verbs
> - adverbs

Challenge 1

1. Underline the **modal verb** in each sentence below.

   a) The other team will be hard to beat as they've been training hard.

   b) Freddy can play piano and guitar to a very high standard.

   c) Jess knows she should phone her grandparents more often.

   d) The teacher says we can have an extended playtime.

   [ ] 4 marks

2. Sort each verb you have underlined in Question 1 above into the table below.

Shows a degree of certainty	Shows an obligation	Shows ability	Shows permission

   [ ] 4 marks

Challenge 2

1. Underline the most suitable **modal verb** to complete each sentence below.

   a) I **can / must** speak two foreign languages because I've lived in Italy and France.

   b) Mum said Sal **can / must** have a sore throat as she has coughed all night.

   c) The teacher said we **could / ought to** play either hockey or golf, depending on the weather.

   [ ] 3 marks

2. Underline the **adverbs** in the sentences below that indicate uncertainty.

   a) You should probably leave early today as it looks like it might snow.

   b) If you would only try a bit harder, maybe you'd succeed!

   [ ] 2 marks

Challenge 3

1. Insert a suitable different **adverb** in each sentence below to indicate certainty.

   a) Taking exercise is _____ good for your health.

   b) Joe had _____ eaten his breakfast, judging by the amount of crumbs on the table.

   [ ] 2 marks

Total: [   ] / 15 marks

Had a go [ ]   **Getting there** [ ]   **Got it!** [ ]

Progress test 2

1. Write the underlined words in the **present perfect tense**.

   a) Dad <u>built</u> _____ an extension on the back of our house.

   b) Some thoughtless people <u>dropped</u> _____ litter in the woods.

   c) Mr Martin <u>went</u> _____ to a teachers' conference.

   d) A swarm of bees <u>flew</u> _____ towards the hives.

   4 marks

2. Underline the two **command verbs** in each sentence below.

   a) Bring me your test papers, please, but first check you have written your name at the top.

   b) Stick a stamp on the envelope then take the letter to the post office please.

   c) Turn left at the end of the road, then go first right.

   d) Please look under the mat and see if you can find the spare key.

   8 marks

3. What is the **word class** of the underlined word below?

   "I've had a <u>really</u> difficult start to the day because the car wouldn't start," complained Dad.

   _____

   1 mark

4. Rewrite the verb in bold in each sentence below in the **present progressive tense**.

   a) Maya **watches** the Wimbledon tennis final with her mum.   _____

   b) We **paint** a picture of a bowl of fruit.   _____

   c) Felipe **hopes** his team gets at least a draw today.   _____

   d) Mum **brushes** the leaves up before she cuts the grass.   _____

   4 marks

5. Underline the subordinate clause in each sentence below.

   a) I enjoyed the book although it was hard to understand the plot.

   b) As we knew it was going to be a long journey, we packed a big lunch.

c) Isabella wore her waterproof coat even though it wasn't raining.

d) The children were told what to do if the fire alarm started ringing.

4 marks

6. Underline all the **determiners** in the sentence below.

In science, we studied the different features of some minibeasts that we found under a plank.

3 marks

7. Rewrite the sentence below so that it starts with the **adverbial**.

We finished our science experiment before lunch.

_____

2 marks

8. Rewrite the sentence below so that it does **not** contain a **relative pronoun.**

The car that we bought a few years ago appears to have a fault with its engine.

_____

_____

1 mark

9. Replace each underlined word with a pronoun in the box below.

The plumber has come to fix the tap. The plumber has promised to fix the tap within the hour.

2 marks

10. Underline the verbs that are in the **past progressive tense** in the sentences below.

a) I was waiting ages for the bus, which had been held up due to an accident.

b) As we were planning our visit to the leisure centre, Mum got a call to say it was closed.

c) Dad was washing the dishes when he smashed Mum's favourite glass.

d) Although we didn't see anything suspicious, our dog was barking all night.

4 marks

11. Rewrite these sentences in the **passive voice.**

a) The train conductor collected our fares.

_____

b) The fireman rescued the cat from the top of the tree.

_____

c) An excellent local company re-covered our old armchair.

_____

d) Mum planned our kitchen extension.

_____

4 marks

12. Rewrite the sentences below in the **active voice**.

   a) We were attacked by a swarm of bees as we were eating our picnic.

_____

_____

   b) The celebrity was escorted through the crowd by officials.

_____

_____

2 marks

13. **Tick a box in each row to show whether each sentence contains a relative pronoun, a coordinating conjunction or a subordinating conjunction.**

Sentence	Relative pronoun	Coordinating conjunction	Subordinating conjunction
Stanley is good in all subject areas, but he performs best in English.			
Our teacher, whose dog recently had pups, showed us a video of them playing.			
Although it's a sunny day, the wind is actually very cold.			

3 marks

14. Rewrite the statement below so that it is a **question**.

Enrico has studied hard for his piano exam.

_____

1 mark

15. Underline the **relative clause** in each sentence below.

a) The cake that I baked is chocolate with a blackberry jam filling.

b) We have just watched a comedy film, which has really cheered us up.

c) Our vegetable patch, where the garden slopes slightly downhill, is thriving.

3 marks

16. Explain the difference in meaning between the two sentences below.

Dragonflies were on Earth for around 300 million years.

Dragonflies have been on Earth for around 300 million years.

Sentence 1: _____

Sentence 2: _____

2 marks

17. Complete each sentence by writing the verbs in brackets in the **past perfect tense.**

a) Sian (draw) _____ the curtains against the dark night when she heard a knock at the door.

b) Ryan successfully reached the summit even though he (lose)

_____ some time due to the snowstorm.

2 marks

18. What is the **function** of the sentence below?

How impressive that live performance was last night

Tick **one.**

statement ☐   exclamation ☐

question ☐   command ☐

1 mark

Total: ☐ / 51 marks

45

Punctuation: commas

- Use commas correctly in lists
- Use commas to avoid ambiguity
- Use commas after fronted adverbials
- Use commas after fronted subordinate clauses

Commas in lists

Commas can be used to separate items in a list. In most lists, there is no comma after the last item in the list and the word 'and'.

Example

Our holiday clothes consisted of sandals, shorts, sun-hats and swimming costumes.

Commas to avoid ambiguity

Commas can be used to avoid ambiguity, to make the intended meaning clear.

Example

Freya's hobbies are cooking, her tortoise and reading.

Without the **comma**, this sentence would be:

Freya's hobbies are cooking her tortoise and reading.

Commas after fronted adverbials

Commas are used after fronted adverbials.

Example

After school, I usually play football on the field before I go home.

Commas after subordinate clauses

If a sentence starts with a subordinate clause, it is followed by a **comma**.

Example

Miles wore his gloves although it wasn't that cold.

Although it wasn't that cold, Miles wore his gloves.

> **Tip**
>
> Take a brief pause when you see a comma when you are reading.

> **Remember**
>
> In most lists, there is no comma after the last list item and the word 'and'.

> **Tip**
>
> Ambiguity is a reference to something that could have more than one meaning and therefore could cause confusion.

> **Key Words**
>
> - comma
> - ambiguity
> - fronted adverbial
> - subordinate clause

1. Add **three commas** to each sentence below.

   a) Alfie consulted the recipe book and noted that he would need sultanas sugar eggs plain flour and cherries.

   b) We have seen a wide range of weather this week: sunshine gales hailstones fog and blizzards.

   c) Mum has been planting seeds; she hopes to have home-grown aubergines chillies tomatoes beetroot and carrots in the summer months.

9 marks

Challenge 2

1. Explain how a **comma** changes the meaning of the second sentence below.

   Bethan asked if Maggie Bailey and Luca would help her set up the hall for PE.

   Bethan asked if Maggie, Bailey and Luca would help her set up the hall for PE.

   _____

1 mark

2. Insert a **comma** in each sentence below.

   Before school I usually sit in the library with my book.

   During the summer we went on a camping trip to Devon.

2 marks

Challenge 3

1. Rewrite the sentence below so that it starts with the **subordinate clause**.

   My grandparents are excellent climbers even though they are in their seventies.

   _____

   _____

2 marks

2. Insert a **comma** in the sentence below to show that only Zayn and Chris went to the park.

   After they left James Zayn and Chris went to the park.

1 mark

3. Insert **two commas** in the sentence below to show that James, Zayn **and** Chris all went to the park.

   After they left James Zayn and Chris went to the park.

2 marks

Total: [ ] / 17 marks

Had a go [ ]   **Getting there** [ ]   **Got it!** [ ]

47

Punctuation: inverted commas

- Use inverted commas correctly in direct speech

Inverted commas

Inverted commas, sometimes called speech marks, are used to indicate direct speech. They come at the start and end of the spoken words. The closing **inverted commas** come *after* the final punctuation mark at the end of the direct speech.

Tip

Inverted commas can either be "double" or 'single' but don't mix the two!

Example

> closing inverted comma comes *after* the comma

'There's enough snow to make a snowman,' Jaime said.

'Shall we use a carrot for his nose?' asked Anna.

'Good idea,' replied Jaime, 'and stones for his nose and eyes?'

Be careful when rewriting direct speech as indirect speech. You will need to change some words.

Example

'I'll be late,' said Levy. → Levy said he would be late.

Inverted commas can also be used when you quote from a text or a speech.

Example

In the deep silence of the still countryside, the only interruption was an occasional passing train, a reminder that there was another life in the towns and cities beyond.

Question: What is the impact of 'an occasional passing train'? Give evidence from the text to support your answer.

Answer: The noise of the train interrupts 'the deep silence of the still countryside.'

Remember

Opening inverted commas should look like back-to-front commas and closing inverted commas should look like normal commas. They should be positioned at the same height as any capital letters or tall letters in the direct speech.

Inverted commas can be used when referring to a book or film title, or to show a nickname.

Example

Last night, we saw 'The Lion King' at the theatre.

I call my brother 'The Destroyer' because he's clumsy.

Key Words

- inverted commas
- speech marks
- direct speech
- indirect speech

Challenge 1

1. Tick two boxes to show where the missing **inverted commas** should go.

I've just discovered that our cousins are coming for the weekend, said Brogan.

☐   ☐   ☐   ☐

☐ 2 marks

2. Tick the sentence below that is punctuated correctly.

Tick one.

'I've just seen Bertie walking his new dog'! exclaimed Mia.   ☐

'I've just seen Bertie walking his new dog! exclaimed Mia.'   ☐

'I've just seen Bertie walking his new dog!' exclaimed Mia.   ☐

I've just seen Bertie walking his new dog! exclaimed Mia.   ☐

☐ 1 mark

Challenge 2

1. Insert the missing **inverted commas** in the direct speech below.

a) How many items are on today's agenda? asked the Year 6 House Captain.

b) Please help me peel the carrots, said Mum, otherwise dinner will be very late.

☐ 3 marks

2. Rewrite the following sentence as **direct speech**.

Sam told his sister he would help her with her homework.

_____

☐ 1 mark

Challenge 3

1. Insert the five missing pairs of **inverted commas** in the passage below.

I've just read an article called Life in the Palace about the Queen. One source said: Her Majesty is always in bed by 10pm. Another said: Her Majesty likes cereal and toast for breakfast. My favourite quote was by the palace dog trainer who revealed: Her Majesty likes to curl up with her dogs on the sofa while she watches a programme called Walkies on TV.

☐ 5 marks

Total: ☐ / 12 marks

Had a go ☐   **Getting there** ☐   **Got it!** ☐

Punctuation: apostrophes

- Use apostrophes correctly in contractions
- Use apostrophes correctly to indicate both singular and plural possession

Apostrophes in contractions

Apostrophes can be used in writing **contractions**; these are shortened forms of words from which one or more letters have been left out. The apostrophe is positioned exactly above where the missing letter, or letters, would be.

Example

I am → I'm

> Here, the apostrophe indicates the missing letter 'a'.

Remember

We tend to use contractions when we speak or write informally.

Apostrophes for possession

Apostrophes can be used to show that something belongs to someone. To show **possession** in singular nouns, the apostrophe comes after the word followed by the letter 's'.

Example

a lady's handbag   Mum's boss's husband

Tip

The apostrophe is shaped like a comma. It sits at the same height as any capital letters or tall letters in the sentence.

To show possession in plural nouns, the **apostrophe** comes *after* the letter 's' that makes the noun plural.

Example

the ladies' handbags   my sisters' friends

the dogs' biscuits   Mum's bosses' husbands

Remember

The word 'it's' is always a contraction of 'it is'. When using 'its' to show possession, there is no apostrophe. For example, 'The dog wagged its tail'.

To show possession in irregular plural nouns, the **apostrophe** comes after the plural noun and *before* the letter 's'.

Example

the men's changing rooms   the children's lacrosse match

For proper nouns ending in the letter 's', usually an apostrophe is added followed by the letter 's'. However, you may also see an apostrophe with no letter 's'.

Key Words

- apostrophe
- contraction
- possession

Example

James's pen OR James' pen   Jess's shoes OR Jess' shoes

Challenge 1

1. Tick one box in each row to say whether the **apostrophe** in each sentence is used in a contraction or to indicate possession.

Sentence	Contraction	Possession
My sister's making me a bowl of soup.		
Our class's representative is Mariam.		
Ben was sure he'd brought his homework.		
The police found the thieves' footsteps.		

4 marks

Challenge 2

1. Write the contracted forms of the following words.

was not   _____   I would   _____

we will   _____   they had   _____

should have   _____   shall not   _____

they are   _____   will not   _____

8 marks

Challenge 3

1. Rewrite each sentence so that it uses an **apostrophe** to show possession.

The books belonging to the girls are overdue.

_____

The crown belonging to the princess is studded with diamonds and rubies.

_____

2 marks

2. Add an **apostrophe** to the word 'its' where needed in the passage below.

Its with no small amount of fear that we creep through the forest, not wanting to wake the beast from **its** sleep. We know **its** in **its** cave but **its** bound to hear us if we aren't careful. **Its** almost dark now so **its** best we find shelter before **its** too late.

6 marks

Total: ____ / 20 marks

Had a go ☐   Getting there ☐   Got it! ☐

Punctuation: parenthesis

- Use brackets, dashes and commas correctly to indicate parenthesis in a sentence

Parenthesis

Parenthesis refers to a word or phrase inserted into a sentence as an explanation or an afterthought. The punctuation marks used to demarcate the parenthesis can be **brackets**, **dashes** or **commas**.

Brackets

Brackets can come in the middle of a sentence or at the end.

Example

It was 2am (I know because I checked my watch) when I heard frantic knocking on the front door.

We ate the stale sandwich and quickly left the restaurant (we won't be going back there in a hurry).

Dashes

A pair of **dashes** can also demarcate the word or words in parenthesis.

Example

The teacher was cross – not surprisingly – as we had pushed her patience to the limit.

One of my best friends – Harry – is brilliant at football.

Commas

A pair of **commas** can also demarcate the word or words in parenthesis.

Example

We were on holiday, camping in Devon, when we heard the good news.

Freya, who's usually very timid, amazed us with her courage when the boat capsized.

> **Remember**
>
> When you take the word or words that are in parenthesis out of the sentence, what is left still makes sense – it is a main clause.

> **Tip**
>
> A dash is twice the length of a hyphen (see page 56).

> **Key Words**
>
> - parenthesis
> - brackets
> - dashes
> - commas

Challenge 1

1. Which sentence below uses brackets correctly to show **parenthesis**?

Tick **one**.

My brother Miles the one (who's mad about music)
is going to a concert tonight.

My brother Miles (the one who's mad about music)
is going to a concert tonight.

My brother Miles the one who's mad (about music)
is going to a concert tonight.

My brother Miles (the one who's mad about music
is going to a concert) tonight.

1 mark

Challenge 2

1. Which grammatical term describes the words in **parenthesis** in the sentence below?

My uncle Ravi, who is sportier than Dad, is taking me to the climbing centre later.

Tick **one**.

adverbial phrase

relative clause

prepositional phrase

noun phrase

1 mark

Challenge 3

1. Insert dashes to show **parenthesis** in each sentence below.

   a) Following the match, we went home tired and muddy to a bowl of hot soup.

   b) Marco tightrope walker extraordinaire amazed the crowd with his daring agility.

2 marks

2. Insert suitable punctuation so that there is **parenthesis** in each sentence below.

   a) Luckily, Dana with only seconds to spare managed to get the last train home.

   b) We cheered when the trapeze artists with extraordinary agility swapped in mid-air.

2 marks

Total: [ ] / 6 marks

Had a go [ ]   **Getting there** [ ]   **Got it!** [ ]

Punctuation: colons and semi-colons

- Use a colon between two clauses, to introduce lists, and before a quotation
- Use a semi-colon to link two closely related sentences and to separate longer items in lists

Colons

A **colon** can be used after a clause, to **introduce another clause** that explains or gives more detail about the first clause.

Colons can also be used to **introduce lists**, to **introduce a quotation** and in play scripts to **introduce lines**.

Tip

In play scripts, there are no inverted commas around the characters' spoken words.

Example

Finding the answer to the puzzle wasn't easy: the clues left by the mysterious stranger were hard to solve.

> colon introducing another clause

Our timetable today includes the following: maths, English, science, history and art.

> colon introducing a list

The headline in the educational article said: 'Grasping Grammar is Great!'

> colon introducing a quotation

Juliet: O Romeo, Romeo, wherefore art thou Romeo?

> colon introducing a character's lines in a play script

Semi-colons

A **semi-colon** can be used instead of a full stop to link two closely related independent clauses.

Semi-colons can also be used to separate items in a list where the items themselves contain commas. This avoids confusion that may arise from too many commas.

Example

I love visiting the Lake District; the views are spectacular.

When we were on holiday, we met a couple from Belfast, Northern Ireland; Elsa from Munich, Germany, and her friend from Amsterdam, Holland; and Madeleine, Audrey and Dion from Morzine in the French Alps.

Key Words

- colon
- semi-colon

Challenge 1

1. Which sentence below uses a **semi-colon** correctly?

Tick **one**.

Suzie enjoys an outdoor lifestyle she has; a lovely garden, a fire pit and a barbecue. ☐

When she invites friends round, they know; they'll be sitting outside she has plenty of spare fleeces and provides blankets for everyone. ☐

Last time I visited, she made veggie burgers and salad; we sat outside and talked until the sun went down. ☐

I'm hoping she will have a party for her birthday next week the forecast is; very good. ☐

☐ 1 mark

Challenge 2

1. Insert a **colon** in the correct place in each sentence below.

a) We need to pack the following for our trip to the seaside swimming costumes, goggles, snorkels, masks and flippers.

b) The Head Teacher made her last announcement of the evening tea and coffee would be served in the staffroom.

c) For our art lesson today, we will need a range of equipment scissors, glue, paper, paints and water.

d) There was clearly only one thing to do report the incident to the police and let them take action.

☐ 4 marks

Challenge 3

1. Insert **one colon** and **three semi-colons** in the passage below.

My favourite books are the following 'Harry Potter and the Philosopher's Stone' and 'Harry Potter and the Goblet of Fire', both by J K Rowling 'Absolutely Everything' by Christopher Lloyd, which is great for dipping into and 'The Boy at the Back of the Class' by Anjari Rauf. 'A Boy Called Hope' by Lara Williamson is an interesting read about family relationships and friendships I should have finished it by next week.

☐ 4 marks

Total: ☐ / **9 marks**

Had a go ☐   **Getting there** ☐   **Got it!** ☐

Punctuation: single dashes, hyphens and bullet points

- Use a dash to indicate additional information to a preceding clause
- Use a dash for dramatic effect, to signal an interruption or a change in direction
- Use a hyphen in some compound words and to join prefixes to some words
- Use bullet points in non-fiction texts

Dashes

A single **dash** can be used at the start of a clause, adding extra information to the preceding clause. It can also be used for dramatic effect, to signal an interruption or change in direction.

Tip

A dash might replace a semi-colon or a colon.

Example

There was a rainforest, fresh water and exotic fruits – everything the explorers had hoped for could be found on the island.

The jury finally decided on the verdict – guilty.

'Ryan, do you think you could – oh never mind, I'll do it.'

Hyphens

A **hyphen** can join two words to make a **compound word**, to act as an **adjective** before a **noun**, and thus avoid **ambiguity**.

A hyphen can also be used to join a **prefix** to a word where the meaning would be ambiguous without it.

A hyphen is often used when a prefix ending with a vowel is added to a word starting with a vowel.

Key Words

- dash
- hyphen
- compound word
- ambiguity
- prefix
- bullet points

Example

heavy + metal → heavy-metal detector

re-cover → Gran had her armchair re-covered.

recover → Gran has recovered from her illness.

co-operate   co-ordinate   no-one

Without the **hyphen**, the phrase would read as though the metal detector itself is 'heavy', rather than a detector that finds heavy metals.

Bullet points

Bullet points are often used in non-fiction to highlight important information. They usually come after an introductory sentence that ends with a colon.

The text following each bullet point does not need to start with a capital letter or end with a full stop.

Example

You must visit:

- Buckingham Palace
- St Paul's Cathedral
- Big Ben

Challenge 1

1. Insert a **dash** in each sentence below.

   a) We had reached the mountain's summit or had we?

   b) There was only one thing for it sink or swim.

   c) 'I wanted *Sami* to come swimming with me not *you!*' moaned Freddie.

   d) The maths paper was very hard so hard that I think I've failed.

   4 marks

Challenge 2

1. Insert a **hyphen** in each sentence so that it contains a compound word acting as an adjective.

   a) Auntie Sal only drinks sugar free cola and lemonade.

   b) Vadim has been a hard working man all his life.

   c) After the argument and a soul searching evening, Clara realised she'd been wrong.

   3 marks

Challenge 3

1. Insert **two dashes** in the sentence below to show the dramatic effect of Jamil opening the front door.

   'It can't be it is yes, it's really you!' exclaimed Jamil when he opened the front door.

   1 mark

2. Explain the different meaning of each word in bold in the sentences below.

   The lawyer made an error when signing the paperwork so he **re-signed** it.

   The lawyer **resigned** from the company as he had made too many errors.

   re-signed _____

   resigned _____

   2 marks

Total: ☐ / 10 marks

Had a go ☐   **Getting there** ☐   **Got it!** ☐

Formal and informal speech and writing

- Distinguish between formal and informal language
- Distinguish between Standard and non-Standard English
- Use the subjunctive verb form in formal speech and writing

Formal and informal language

Formal speech and writing are used in 'serious' contexts such as delivering a speech, applying for a job or writing to your head teacher. **Standard English** is always used; this means using correct grammar.

Example

> Good evening, ladies and gentlemen. I would like to extend a very warm welcome to you all. May I commence by saying how strongly I feel about the issue of pollution, something you will witness in my forthcoming speech in which I intend to win you round to my point of view.

The **subjunctive form** might be used in formal speech and writing, often in a **subordinate clause**.

Example

> Before I start, I need to draw your attention to some safety rules. If there **were** to be a fire, an alarm bell will sound.

Subjunctive form

Informal speech and writing is a relaxed, 'chatty' way of communicating with family and friends, often using slang and contracted words. **Standard English** should still be used.

Example

> Hiya, how's it goin'? You goin' to footie practice later?

> Nah, can't be bothered. Got loadsa homework.

Non-standard English means speech and writing that is grammatically incorrect.

Example

> Have you seen where I put them books?

> No, but I seen them yesterday.

Remember

Standard English should always be used in both formal and informal speech and writing.

Contractions such as 'I'd' tend to be avoided.

More formal vocabulary is used, e.g. 'commence' instead of 'start'.

Tip

The subjunctive verb form can also be used to express a wish, e.g. *I wish I **were** lying on a sunny beach!* or an imaginary state, e.g. *If only she **were** rich!*

Tip

Informal writing might be used when writing postcards, diary entries and texts.

Key Words

- formal speech/writing
- Standard English
- subjunctive form
- informal speech/writing
- non-Standard English

Challenge 1

1. Tick one box in each row to show whether you would use **formal** or **informal** speech and writing for each of the genres shown.

Genre	Formal	Informal
A text to your friend		
A letter to the local council		
A postcard to a cousin		
Your diary entry		
A speech for a debate in which you are participating		
An email to a sibling		

6 marks

Challenge 2

1. Rewrite the following sentences using **Standard English**.

   a) We ain't going to the park – we got visitors.

   _____

   b) Pick them shoes up or I'll be well cross.

   _____

   c) Hayley would of helped you if you would of asked her.

   _____

6 marks

Challenge 3

1. Underline the sentence that is most **formal** in the passage below.

   Hear you've been a bit unwell lately. Such a shame but hopefully you're a bit better now. If this is not the case, a doctor ought to be contacted. Send me a quick text to let me know how you're doing.

1 mark

2. Complete the sentence so that it is in the **subjunctive form**.

   If Mr Robertson _____ to arrive early, please escort him to my office.

1 mark

Total: ☐ / 14 marks

Had a go ☐	Getting there ☐	Got it! ☐

Progress test 3

1. Insert **four commas** in the sentence below.

   Our history teacher said we would be exploring the lives of Catherine of Aragon Anne Boleyn Jane Seymour Anne of Cleves Catherine Howard and Catherine Parr.

   `4 marks`

2. Rewrite the sentence below so that it starts with the **subordinate clause**.

   We're really looking forward to the school fair although the forecast isn't great.

   _____

   _____

   `2 marks`

3. Which sentence uses **apostrophes** for contraction correctly?

   Tick **one**.

   Ive' not had my holiday yet because my dads' been too busy at work. ☐

   We'll probably go to the caravan where ther'es always so much to do. ☐

   Our cousin's coming to join us so that'll be fun. ☐

   There's not really anywhere else Iw'd rather be. ☐

   `1 mark`

4. Complete each sentence using the underlined words in the **present perfect tense**.

   a) Mum <u>looked</u> _____ everywhere for her keys.

   b) Some children <u>leave</u> _____ their PE kit in school.

   c) Miles <u>went</u> _____ to a concert.

   d) James <u>threw</u> _____ the ball to Cerys.

   `4 marks`

5. Insert a **comma** in each sentence below.

   a) In future you really should check you've brought your PE kit with you.

   b) Every afternoon our teacher reads to us from our class novel.

   `2 marks`

6. Insert suitable punctuation to show the words that are in **parenthesis** in the sentence below.

   We went white-water rafting an often dangerous sport and thoroughly enjoyed ourselves.

   `1 mark`

7. Underline the **subject** and circle the **object** in the sentence below.

My cousin Jack lives in a cottage next to the sea.

2 marks

8. Insert a **dash** in each sentence below.

a) I had reached the end of my magical adventure or so I thought.

b) I turned the corner and surveyed the scene a horror that words could not describe!

2 marks

9. Write a sentence using each word below.

> a) represent   b) re-present

a) _____

b) _____

2 marks

10. Insert a **semi-colon** in each sentence below.

a) The judge's decision was final Sarena was undoubtedly the clear winner.

b) When we go hiking, we take a flask of coffee it warms us up in the winter months.

2 marks

11. Underline **two adjectives** in the sentence below.

Dad's car may be ancient but it is reliable, and gets us where we need to go.

2 marks

12. Tick one box on each row to show the **tense** of the underlined verbs in each sentence.

Sentence	Present perfect	Past perfect	Present progressive	Past progressive
Phillip <u>has decided</u> to buy a new house after much consideration.				
Sammie <u>is studying</u> the works of a famous artist.				
I was sure that I <u>had handed</u> my homework in.				
You <u>were sleeping</u> when I phoned you.				

4 marks

61

13. **Rewrite the sentences below so that they are in Standard English.**

   a) We was at the cinema when we seen a flashing light.

   _____

   b) It could of been a police car or a ambulance.

   _____

   c) We wasn't worried but hoped it weren't nothing serious.

   _____

   d) When we come out, we didn't see nothing odd.

   _____

   8 marks

14. **Insert a hyphen in each sentence so that it contains a compound word acting as an adjective.**

   a) Maria is a sensible, quick thinking girl who can be trusted at all times.

   b) My little brother may be forgetful, annoying and accident prone but he has a heart of gold.

   c) On the long journey to Grandma's, Dad called into a self service café so we could have a snack.

   d) Verity is very bad tempered in the mornings but by lunchtime she is laughing and joking.

   4 marks

15. **Underline the word in the passage below that uses an apostrophe for possession.**

   I think it's going to rain. While we're waiting for better weather, why don't we go to Mo's?

   1 mark

16. **Underline all the determiners in the sentences below.**

   a) We have just been to the theatre to see a really great show.

   b) There were some great performances and two amazing singers!

   2 marks

17. Which sentence below uses **a dash** correctly?

We clambered to the top and fell into each other's arms now – we could celebrate!

We clambered to the top and fell – into each other's arms now we could celebrate!

We clambered to the top and fell into each other's arms – now we could celebrate!

We clambered to the top – and fell into each other's arms now we could celebrate!

1 mark

18. Insert the missing inverted commas in the sentence below.

Please place your test papers on my desk and line up quietly for lunch, said the teacher.

1 mark

19. Insert the missing **apostrophe** to show possession in each sentence below.

a) After many days of searching, Millies PE kit was eventually found in the lost-property cupboard.

b) As I neared my journeys end, I felt excited about seeing my family and friends again.

c) Our two cats beds are in the corner of the utility room, next to the boiler.

d) The princesses gowns were kept in glass wardrobes in each of their bedrooms.

4 marks

20. Write D or H in each box to indicate whether each arrow is pointing to a **dash** or a **hyphen**.

Auntie Freida likes low-fat yoghurt – she's watching her weight.

2 marks

21. Underline **two prepositions** in each sentence below.

a) Monty buried his bone in the garden then two minutes later dug it up again.

b) Finley usually sits beside Katie at the front table.

4 marks

Total: ⬚ / 55 marks

63

Vocabulary: synonyms and antonyms

- Find a synonym for a given word
- Find an antonym for a given word
- Add a negative prefix to a word to form its antonym

Synonyms

A **synonym** is a word with the same or similar meaning as another word.

Example

'Please tidy up the mess you have made,' Tyler **asked**.

'Pick that up immediately,' Kate **commanded**.

'Please come home in ten minutes,' Syed **requested**.

'Please take me to the park,' Joe **pleaded**.

> The verbs *asked*, *commanded*, *requested* and *pleaded* are synonyms.

> **Remember**
>
> When using a dictionary to look for a **synonym**, make sure it is suitable for the context in which you are writing.

Antonyms

An **antonym** is a word that is opposite in meaning to another word.

Example

Maxine is **tall** but her best friend Nadine is **short**.

Here, the river is **narrow** but further downstream it is **wide**.

Although the shops are **open** today, tomorrow they are **closed**.

> **Tip**
>
> Use synonyms in your writing to avoid repeating words.

Some **antonyms** are formed by adding a **negative prefix**.
Negative prefixes include:

de, un, im, in, ir, il, dis, mis

Example

I **agreed** with Martha about the book but George **dis**agreed with both of us.

Sabina's high heels were **im**practical for a wet, muddy walk. Fortunately, I was wearing more **practical** walking boots!

I am good at learning **regular** spellings but I sometimes struggle with **ir**regular spellings.

> **Key Words**
>
> - synonym
> - antonym
> - negative prefix

Challenge 1

1. Find an **antonym** for each adjective below. Use a dictionary to help you.

Adjective	Antonym
weak	
messy	
energetic	
bright	
extrovert	

5 marks

Challenge 2

1. Replace the words in bold with a suitable **synonym**.

   'How **inviting** the sea looks!' said Joseph. _____

   'I'm really **keen** to go for a swim.' _____

   2 marks

2. Replace the word in bold with an **antonym**.

   We **erected** the tent in the back garden. _____

   1 mark

3. Add a negative prefix to each word below to form its **antonym**.

   _____regard   _____proper   _____audible

   3 marks

Challenge 3

1. Which **two words** in the passage below are **synonyms**?

   Our head teacher has always been industrious, reliable and kind. He has made such a difference to our school over the last twenty years. We can only hope his replacement is as hard-working.

   _____   _____

   2 marks

2. Which **two words** in the passage below are **antonyms**?

   Matthew could see only the disadvantage in taking the old car for their trip abroad. There was no guarantee it would get them from London to Paris in its current state, plus the benefit of travelling by train was that they could stretch their legs and have a nap on the way.

   _____   _____

   2 marks

Total: ☐ / 15 marks

| Had a go ☐ | Getting there ☐ | Got it! ☐ |

Vocabulary: prefixes

- Add a prefix to a word to change its meaning
- Identify prefixes with a negative meaning
- Use knowledge of prefix meanings to work out meanings of whole words

Prefixes

A **prefix** is a letter or letters added to the beginning of a word to turn it into another word. The spelling of the original word does not change.

Example

- The prefix 're' means to repeat or to do again:

  recycle   reheat   rewrite   reconstruct

- The **prefix** 'over' implies 'too much':

  overcook   overrun   overeat   overjoyed

Some **prefixes** give the word a negative or opposite meaning.

Example

distasteful   misguided

illegal   irregular

impractical   inactive

untie   decompose

Some **prefixes** have their origins in Greek and Latin. For example, 'bi' which means 'two'; 'tele' which means 'far off'; 'auto' which means 'self'; 'anti' which means 'opposite'; and 'super' which means 'greater' or 'above'.

Example

bicycle   television

anticlockwise   supermarket

autobiography

Tip

If the **root word** starts with 'm' or 'p', use the prefix 'im'. Otherwise, use 'in'.

Tip

If the root word starts with 'l', use the prefix 'il'. If the root word starts with 'r', the prefix 'ir' is generally used.

Remember

A root word is a word on its own, the basic form, before any prefix or suffix is added.

Remember

Some prefixes are used to join a prefix to a word with a hyphen, where the meaning would be ambiguous without it.

Key Words

- prefix
- root word

1. Draw lines to match each **prefix** with a word on the right.

in   responsible

mis   ability

il   respectful

dis   logical

ir   inform

5 marks

1. Complete the table below. The first one has been done for you.

Root word	Word with prefix	Definition of word with prefix
cover	*recover*	*To get well again*
	discover	
appear		To go missing
	reappear	
graph		A person's signature
	autopilot	

8 marks

1. What is the meaning of each **prefix** below?

a) semi   e.g. semi-detached; semi-circle _____

b) sub   e.g. subway; submarine   _____

c) uni   e.g. uniform; unicycle   _____

d) mono   e.g. monotone; monorail   _____

4 marks

Total: [   ] / 17 marks

Had a go [ ]   **Getting there** [ ]   **Got it!** [ ]

Spelling: the *shus* sound spelt '-cious' or '-tious'; the *shul* sound spelt '-cial' or '-tial'

- Spell suffixes with the same sounds correctly

Suffixes

A **suffix** is a letter or letters added to the end of a word, changing its meaning. For example, a **noun** can be changed into an **adjective** by adding a **suffix**.

The sound 'shus' at the end of a word can be spelt '-cious' or '-tious'.

- If the **root word** ends in 'ce', the **suffix** '-cious' is usually used.

- If a related word ends in 'tion', the **suffix** '-tious' is usually used.

Example

Noun	Adjective
vice	vicious
infection	infectious
grace	gracious
caution	cautious

The sound 'shul' at the end of a word can be spelt '-cial' or '-tial'.

- The **suffix** '-cial' is usually used after a vowel.

- The **suffix** '-tial' is usually used after a consonant.

Example

Noun	Adjective
office	official
part	partial
race	racial
resident	residential

Tip

If the root word ends in 'ce', the 'sh' sound is usually spelt as 'c'.

Remember

The vowels are a, e, i, o, u.

Key Words

- suffix
- root word

1. Choose either the **suffix** '-cious' or '-tious' to turn these nouns into adjectives.

Noun	Adjective	Noun	Adjective
malice		repetition	
ambition		space	
nutrition		vice	

6 marks

1. Choose either the **suffix** '-tial' or '-cial' to turn these nouns into adjectives.
   Two of the words are exceptions to the rule!

Noun	Adjective	Noun	Adjective
president		face	
finance		confidence	
torrent		essence	

6 marks

1. Circle the correct spelling in each pair below.

   suspitious / suspicious   fictitious / ficticious   delicious / delitious

3 marks

2. Change each noun in the box into an **adjective**, then complete each sentence below.

   > suspect   fiction   influence   nutrition

   a) Our school policy is that only _____ food should
      be served.

   b) Mum's charity work has been very _____ in raising
      awareness of the homeless.

   c) On our way to the shops, we saw a _____ character
      lurking on the corner.

   d) The rumours that our teacher was retiring proved to be entirely

      _____.

4 marks

Total: ☐ / 19 marks

| Had a go ☐ | Getting there ☐ | Got it! ☐ |

Spelling: the suffixes '-ant', '-ance', '-ancy'; '-ent', '-ence', '-ency'

- Spell suffixes with the same sounds correctly

Suffixes '-ant', '-ance' and '-ancy'

Use the **suffixes** '-ant', '-ance' and '-ancy' if there is an 'ay' sound before the suffix in a related word.

Example

observe ⟶ observation ⟶ observance

expect ⟶ expectation ⟶ expectant

Suffixes '-ent', '-ence' and '-ency'

Use the **suffixes** '-ent', '-ence' and '-ency' after a soft 'c'; after a soft 'g'; or after 'qu'.

Example

decent / decency

regent / regency

sequence / sequency

Where a verb ends in '-y', '-ure' or '-ear', the noun will take the suffix '-ance'. Where a verb ends in '-ere' or '-er', the noun will take the suffix '-ence'.

Example

ally ⟶ alliance

insure ⟶ insurance

disappear ⟶ disappearance

adhere ⟶ adherence

prefer ⟶ preference

Remember

There are many words which do not follow these spelling rules. You will just have to learn these!

Tip

Some words belong to more than one word class. For example, 'sequence' can be a noun or a verb.

Key Word

- suffix

1. Choose either the **suffix** '-ence' or '-ance' to change these verbs into nouns.

tolerate _____ hesitate _____

dominate _____ observe _____

apply _____ obey _____

1. Complete the table below by adding an appropriate **suffix** to each verb to form an adjective and a noun.

Verb	Adjective	Noun
differ		
resist		
reside		
insist		
buoy		

1. Change the words in the box into **nouns**, then complete each sentence with the appropriate word.

reassure   defend   rely   endure

a) Our trek in the Peak District was a real _____ test!

b) The _____ refused to admit her guilt at the trial.

c) After much _____ from my friends, I confronted the bully in the playground.

d) Stella's _____ on her brother for help with her homework has got to stop.

2. What is the spelling rule for adding the **suffix** '-ance' to the verbs **rely** and **comply**?

_____

Total: [ ] / 16 marks

Had a go [ ]   **Getting there** [ ]   **Got it!** [ ]

Spelling: the suffixes '-able', '-ably'; '-ible', '-ibly'

- Add suffixes to make adjectives and adverbs

Suffixes '-able' and '-ably'

The **suffix** '-able' can be added to a **verb** to make an **adjective**.

Example

understand ⟶ understand**able**

consider ⟶ consider**able**

If the verb ends in 'ce' or 'ge', the 'e' is kept when the suffix is added. This keeps the 'c' or 'g' as a 'soft' sound.

Example

notice ⟶ notic**eable**

change ⟶ chang**eable**

If the verb ends in 'y', change the 'y' to 'i' when adding the suffixes '-able' and '-ably'.

Example

rely ⟶ reli**able** ⟶ reli**ably**

Using the same spelling rules, the suffix '-ably' can be added to a **verb** to make an **adverb**.

Example

understand ⟶ understand**ably**

notice ⟶ notic**eably**

Suffixes '-ible' and '-ibly'

The suffix '-ible' can be added to a **verb** to make an **adjective**, and '-ibly' can be added to make an **adverb**, though they are not as common as the suffixes '-able' and '-ably'.

Example

sense ⟶ sens**ible** ⟶ sens**ibly**

force ⟶ forc**ible** ⟶ forc**ibly**

Tip

Use '-able' and '-ably' if a there is a related word ending in '-ation'. For example, consider ⟶ consider**ation** ⟶ consider**ably**

Tip

Usually, the suffixes '-able' and '-ably' are used if a complete root word can be heard before the suffix. For example, understand**able** / understand**ably**

Remember

Change 'y' to 'i' when adding the suffixes '-able' and '-ably' to verbs ending in 'y'.

Key Words

- suffix
- root word

1. Add the **suffixes** '-able' and '-ably' to the verbs below to make adjectives and adverbs.

	Adjective	**Adverb**
adore	_____	_____
prefer	_____	_____
desire	_____	_____
accept	_____	_____

8 marks

1. Change these verbs into **adjectives**, then complete each sentence below.

> reason   advise   terrify   irritate   access

a) Dad gets _____ if we leave a mess in the kitchen.

b) Our teacher gives us a _____ amount of homework.

c) In the autumn, it is _____ to carry an umbrella.

d) Our caravan site is only _____ from the coast road.

e) Last summer, the weather in Wales was truly _____.

5 marks

1. Underline the correct spelling in each word pair. Use a dictionary to help you.

a) We have a new, much more **fashionable / fashionible** summer uniform.

b) After the kitchen fire, our house was **uninhabitable / uninhabitible**.

c) Although Gwen isn't very **flexable / flexible**, she enjoys her yoga classes.

d) When I am eighteen, I'll be **eligible / eligable** to vote in the election.

4 marks

2. Change the verbs below into **adverbs**.

justify _____   notice _____

rely _____   change _____

4 marks

Total: ☐ / 21 marks

Had a go ☐   **Getting there** ☐   **Got it!** ☐

Spelling: words ending in '-fer'

• Add suffixes starting with a vowel to words ending in '-fer'

Suffixes beginning with a vowel

When a **suffix** beginning with a **vowel** (such as '-ed' or '-ing') is added to a word ending in '-fer', the 'r' is doubled if the 'fer' ending is still **stressed** when the suffix is added.

Example

prefer ⟶ preferred ⟶ preferring

> double 'r' because 'fer' is still stressed

infer ⟶ inferred ⟶ inferring

Say the word out loud to help you identify where the stress (or **emphasis**) falls.

If 'fer' is not stressed after the suffix has been added, the 'r' is not doubled.

Example

prefer ⟶ preference
infer ⟶ inference
buffer ⟶ buffered ⟶ buffering
suffer ⟶ suffered ⟶ suffered

> single 'r' because 'fer' is **not** stressed

Tip

When adding suffixes to words containing 'fer', split them into syllables when saying them, to help you see where the stress falls. This will help you to know whether to double the 'r' or not.

Key Words

• suffix
• stress
• syllable

Challenge 1

1. Say each word in bold out loud to help you decide on the correct spelling in each word pair. Write the correct spellings on the lines below.

   a) Mum carefully **transfered / transferred** the mixture to the cake tin.

   b) Our class has a **preference / preferrence** for science over geography.

   c) The lawyer **confered / conferred** with the judge about the defendant's statement.

   d) Dad's excellent **referrence / reference** was instrumental in him securing his new job.

   _____   _____

   _____   _____

4 marks

Challenge 2

1. Underline the syllable that is stressed in each word containing 'fer'.

   a) I inferred from the text that the character had something to hide.

   b) Sam didn't realise that the teacher was referring to his art work.

   c) The decision has been deferred until the end of the year.

   d) My favourite player is transferring to another club.

4 marks

Challenge 3

1. Add a suitable **suffix** to each word in brackets to complete the sentences below.

   a) Dad produced what Mum called 'a burnt _____' from the oven.   (offer)

   b) Henry's uncle is a firm but fair football _____.
      (refer)

   c) Our head teacher is attending an educational _____.
      (confer)

   d) Molly's painting of the scene _____ from Rav's.
      (differ)

4 marks

Total: [   ] / 12 marks

Had a go [ ]   **Getting there** [ ]   **Got it!** [ ]

Spelling: letter string 'ough'

- Spell words containing the letter string 'ough'
- Know that the letter string 'ough' has different sounds

'ough'

The **letter string** 'ough' is tricky to spell, especially as it can be used to spell a few different sounds.

Example

- enough ← ough pronounced 'uff', as in cuff

- through ← ough pronounced 'oo' as in boo

- dough ← ough pronounced 'oh' as in blow

- brought ← ough pronounced 'aw' as in claw

- bough ← ough pronounced 'ow' as in cow

- cough ← ough pronounced 'o' as in off

To help you remember how to spell the letter string 'ough', think of a **mnemonic**. For example:

o	owls	o	only
u	underestimate	u	ugly
g	greedy	g	giraffes
h	hedgehogs	h	hop

> ### Tip
>
> Try to list as many words as possible that use the 'ough' letter string. Look at a few at a time and try to learn how to pronounce them and how to spell them.

> ### Key Word
>
> - mnemonic

76

Challenge 1

1. Sort the words in the box containing the letter string 'ough' into the correct column in the table below.

> brought   ought   enough   bough   dough   through
>
> thought   plough   fought   trough   bought   tough   although

'ough' pronounced 'uff' (e.g. c**uff**)	'ough' pronounced 'oo' (e.g. b**oo**)	'ough' pronounced 'oh' (e.g. bl**ow**)
'ough' pronounced 'aw' (e.g. cl**aw**)	'ough' pronounced 'ow' (e.g. c**ow**)	'ough' pronounced 'o' (e.g. **off**)

13 marks

Challenge 2

1. Find the **seven** words that have been spelt incorrectly in the passage and write their correct spelling on the lines below.

My brother brawt me some coff mixture because he thawt it would make me better. My throat felt ruff and even the slice of bread I had with my soup had a tuff texture. I know I awt to feel better if I get a good night's sleep but there's no chance of that with the bow of the old oak tree scratching against my window.

_____   _____   _____   _____

_____   _____   _____

7 marks

Challenge 3

1. Choose suitable words from Challenge 1 to complete each sentence below.

   a) The cattle drink from a _____ when they are thirsty.

   b) Dad stretched the pizza _____ before putting it on an oven tray.

   c) The old farmer prefers an old-fashioned horse-drawn _____ to modern-day machinery.

3 marks

Total: ☐ / 23 marks

Had a go ☐	**Getting there** ☐	**Got it!** ☐

Spelling: the digraphs 'ei' and 'ie'

- Spell words with the 'ei' and 'ie' digraphs
- Know that after 'c', the long 'ee' sound is spelt 'ei'
- Know the exceptions to this rule

The digraph 'ei'

The digraph 'ei' can make different sounds.

Example

'ei' with an 'ee' sound ⟶ seize

'ei' with an 'ay' sound ⟶ weigh

'ei' with an 'ih' sound ⟶ sovereign

'ei' with an 'i' sound ⟶ height

After the letter 'c', if the sound made is 'ee', use the **'ei'** digraph.

Example

'ei' with an 'ee' sound after 'c' ⟶ **c**eiling, dec**ei**tful

The digraph 'ie'

The digraph 'ie' can make an 'ee' sound.

Example

field

wield

The same digraph can also make an 'i' sound.

Example

pie

cried

There are some words that just need to be learned!

Example

conscience

ancient

> **Tip**
>
> Sometimes, but not always, the rhyme "*'i' before 'e' except after 'c'*" can help you to spell this digraph.

> **Remember**
>
> There are exceptions to this rule. For example, science.

> **Key Word**
>
> - digraph

Challenge 1

1. Group the words below according to the sound that the digraph **'ei'** makes.

foreign	perceive	height	either	vein	freight
	deceit	protein	caffeine	forfeit	

'ei' after 'c' with an 'ee' sound	'ei' with an 'ee' sound	'ei' with an 'ay' sound	'ei' with an 'ih' sound	'ei' with an 'i' sound

10 marks

Challenge 2

1. Find **ten spelling mistakes** in the passage. Write the correct spelling for each on the lines below.

Niether Sunni nor Grace had done their homework on the Anceint Greeks. Although they knew they would be in trouble, they had siezed the opportunity when the sun came out to sneak out for a walk in the feilds near where they lived. They couldn't beleive it when their nieghbour's dog approached them with a feirce look in his eyes! Grace shreiked but Sunni calmed the dog and they all went home together, where they recieved a breif telling off from their parents.

_____ _____ _____ _____

_____ _____ _____ _____

_____ _____

10 marks

Challenge 3

1. Use the clues to complete the word grids.

a) A female relative.

n				e

b) Proof you have paid for something.

r		c				

c) A pale brown colour.

b				e

d) A substance found in coffee and tea.

c	a							e

4 marks

Total: ___ / 24 marks

Had a go ☐   **Getting there** ☐   **Got it!** ☐

79

Spelling: silent letters

- Spell words with silent letters correctly

Silent letters

Some letters that were pronounced in words hundreds of years ago are no longer sounded today, despite remaining in the words. These letters are called **silent letters**.

Example

The word knight, for example, would once have been pronounced with a hard 'k' sound: k – night.

Even though it is now pronounced without the 'k' sound, its spelling remains as it was originally – with the letter 'k'.

Remember

The study of the origin of words, and the way in which their meanings and sounds have changed throughout history, is called **etymology**.

Patterns with silent letters

There are some patterns that can help you remember how to spell words with silent letters.

Remember

Silent 'k' is always at the beginning of a word, followed by 'n'.

Example

- Silent 'g' is followed by 'n' ⟶ gnat
- Silent 'h' usually follows 'w' or 'r' ⟶ when, rhyme
- Silent 'b' almost always comes at the end of a word, after 'm' ⟶ comb
- Silent 'd' comes before a consonant ⟶ sandwich
- Silent 'n' usually follows 'm' ⟶ autumn
- Silent 's' comes before 'l' ⟶ island
- Silent 't' comes after 's' ⟶ castle
- Silent 'c' comes after 's' ⟶ scene

Tip

Pronouncing the silent letter in your head when saying these words might help you to remember their spelling.

Key Words

- silent letter
- etymology

Challenge 1

1. Underline the **silent letter** in each word below.

hour   solemn   knit   sword   muscle   gnome

6 marks

2. **Four** of the words below are missing their **silent letters**. Identify which ones they are, then write them correctly on the lines below. You might need a dictionary to help you.

physical   silouette   foreign   neumonia   sychology   hym   debt

_____   _____   _____   _____

4 marks

Challenge 2

1. Find the word in each sentence below that is missing its **silent letter**. Rewrite the word correctly on the line on the right. You might need a dictionary to help you.

a) Despite the josling crowd, I managed to get on the train. _____

b) Sighing, Gregor succumed to the rush hour traffic. _____

c) Clicking her narled fingers, the old witch cast her spell. _____

3 marks

Challenge 3

1. Use the clues to complete the crossword.

Across

3. Transports people
5. A quadrilateral with 4 sides the same length.
7. A joint in the finger.
9. Egyptians were buried in one of these.
10. The joint between your hand and arm.

Down

1. Something you do with your ears.
2. A person who fits and repairs water pipes.
4. Truthful.
6. A pink coloured, edible fish.
8. To write your name on something.

10 marks

Total: [ ] / 23 marks

Had a go [ ]   **Getting there** [ ]   **Got it!** [ ]

Spelling: homophones and near-homophone

- Explain what homophones and near-homophones are
- Match given words to their homophone or near-homophone

Homophones

A **homophone** is a word that sounds the same as another word but has a different spelling and meaning.

Example

hair	Myra brushes her hair every morning.
hare	The dog chased the hare into the hedge.
through	Ben walked through the door.
threw	I threw the ball to my friend.

Near-homophones

A **near-homophone** is a word that sounds *almost* the same as another word (but has a different spelling and meaning), which means they are often misspelt.

Example

quiet	We were very quiet when we did our test.
quite	Freya is quite noisy during PE lessons.

Knowing different **word classes** will help you with your spelling of some near-homophones.

Example

advice	Mum gave Dad some advice about his job.

advice – noun

advise	We were glad that Mum was able to advise Dad about his job.

advise – verb

Remember

If you don't use the correct homophone, it could confuse the reader.

Tip

One way to remember how to spell words like **advice** and **advise** is to think of the letter 'c' in 'advice' as being *before* the letter 'n' for noun in the alphabet, and the letter 's' in 'advise' as being *before* the letter 'v' for verb in the alphabet. (This spelling tip will only work if you know the difference between a noun and a verb!)

Key Words

- homophone
- near-homophone

Challenge 1

1. Underline the correct word in each **homophone** pair in bold in the sentences below.

   a) I saw a lovely **pair / pear** of shoes as I **passed / past** the shoe shop.

   b) George had to **pause / paws** the video as he couldn't **bear / bare** to watch the fighting.

   c) As the queen approached the 60th year of her **rein / reign**, the nation **guest / guessed** she would retire.

   d) We aren't **aloud / allowed** to **waist / waste** food as Mum is conscious of those who are starving.

   8 marks

Challenge 2

1. Underline the correct word in each **near-homophone** pair in bold in the passage below.

   It was hard to **except / accept** that our family dog had snapped at our neighbour. I know you should always be **weary / wary** of any animal, but Monty has never been anything **except / accept** gentle and loving. Mum **wanders / wonders** if it might be something to do with the robotic **device / devise** our neighbour was using to cut his grass.

   5 marks

Challenge 3

1. Find **ten** incorrect **homophones** and **near-homophones** in the passage below and write the correct words on the lines provided.

   Since the bus didn't appear dew to a bad accident, we preceded to walk to school. They're was a lot of traffic but we wear careful crossing the roads. In edition to the inconvenience of walking, the whether was dreadful which effected our mood even more. At last, we made the dissent down the hill towards our school wear we new we'd be warm and dry.

   _____ _____ _____ _____

   _____ _____ _____ _____

   _____ _____

   10 marks

   Total: ___ / 23 marks

Had a go ☐   **Getting there** ☐   **Got it!** ☐

Progress test 4

1. Circle the correct spelling in each word pair.

   assurance / assurence   **innocance / innocence**   **frequency / frequancy**

   3 marks

2. Write the underlined words in the **past perfect tense**.

   a) Grace <u>look</u> _____ everywhere for her homework diary.

   b) We <u>thought</u> _____ the film would be better than it turned out.

   2 marks

3. Insert a **semi-colon** in each sentence below.

   a) The trekkers had been planning their trip for many years it was finally a reality.

   b) Gran is desperate for some company we really must visit her this weekend.

   2 marks

4. Choose either '-ence' or '-ance' to change these verbs into **nouns**.

   obey   _____   tolerate   _____

   confide   _____   endure   _____

   4 marks

5. Rewrite the following sentence in the **passive voice**.

   The teachers supervised the children carefully as they climbed up the ropes.

   _____

   _____

   1 mark

6. Underline the **two words** in the passage below that are **synonyms**.

   Joseph's eyes lit up in anticipation of the weekend ahead. Although Mum
   had warned them all of the uncertain weather forecast, there was still an air
   of expectancy in the back of the car.

   1 mark

7. Underline the **two words** in the sentence below that are **antonyms**.

   The children had done a partial clean of the classroom, in the knowledge
   that the cleaners would take a more thorough approach.

   1 mark

8. Complete the passage below after changing the words in the box
   into **nouns**.

   | assist   decent   assure   comply |

   'Your lack of _____ with our school rules is shocking!' scolded the

   teacher. 'I'd like your _____ that this behaviour won't happen again.

   Now, please have the _____ to apologise to the teaching

   _____ who is upset.'

   4 marks

9. Add the **suffix** '-cious' or '-tious', '-cial' or '-tial' to change each noun into an adjective.

Noun	Adjective	Noun	Adjective
part		finance	
infection		president	
vice		office	
space		influence	

8 marks

10. Which sentence below uses a **colon** correctly?

Tick **one**.

I'm telling you: now the man over there in the corner is the lead singer of The Bramble Boys! ☐

I'm telling you now: the man over there in the corner is the lead singer of The Bramble Boys! ☐

I'm telling you now the man over there in the corner is the lead singer of: The Bramble Boys! ☐

I'm telling you now the man over there: in the corner is the lead singer of The Bramble Boys! ☐

1 mark

11. Choose either '-ency' or '-ancy' to change these verbs into **nouns**.

hesitate _____

depend _____

vacate _____

3 marks

12. Find the **six words** that have been spelt incorrectly in the passage. Write their correct spellings on the lines below.

Last weekend, we went camping. On the way there, the weather was unbelievibly horrable. I sulked in the back of the car, feeling incredably disappointed. Dad tried to cheer me up but I put on my headphones and turned up my music so that his voice was inaudable. I fell asleep and when I woke, we had arrived. The weather had changed remarkibly! The sun was shining and there was a warm breeze – it was going to be an unforgettible trip!

_____ _____ _____

_____ _____ _____

6 marks

85

13. Which sentence below uses dashes correctly to show parenthesis?

Tick **one**.

We've been going camping for years – mainly to the east coast – but this year we're off to Wales. ☐

We've been going camping for years mainly – to the east coast – but this year we're off to Wales. ☐

We've been going camping – for years mainly – to the east coast but this year we're off to Wales. ☐

We've been going camping for years mainly to the east coast – but this year we're off – to Wales. ☐

1 mark

14. Find one word in each sentence below that is missing its silent letter. Rewrite the word correctly on the line on the right.

a) The choir sang a solem hymn which echoed round the church.

_____

b) I put my receit safely in my bag and left the shop.

_____

c) We approached the ramparts of the imposing casle and took a photo.

_____

d) Theo is spending the summer on an iland off the coast of Scotland.

_____

4 marks

15. Underline three verbs in the sentence below.

The eagle soared from the clifftop, swooping down to grab its prey from the field below.

3 marks

16. Draw lines to match each prefix with a word on the right.

in	rational
mis	continue
il	active
dis	literate
ir	understand

5 marks

17. Choose either '-ent' or '-ant' to turn these verbs into **adjectives**.

absorb _____   expect _____

excel _____   comply _____

4 marks

18. Use the clues to complete the word grids with words which contain an **'ei'** or an **'ie' digraph**.

a) protect

| s | h | | | | |

b) unbelievable

| i | n | c | o | n | | | | | | l | e |

c) part of something

| p | | | | e |

d) naughtiness

| m | i | s | | | | | |

4 marks

19. Give a **homophone** for each word below.

aisle _____   bridal _____

morning _____   serial _____

profit _____   practise _____

6 marks

20. Give a **near-homophone** for each word below.

desert _____   proceed _____

access _____   addition _____

4 marks

21. Replace each word in bold with a suitable **synonym**. Write your words in the boxes below each.

The **delicate** petals of the flowers had **started** to fade and were **slowly** falling to the ground.

3 marks

Total: _____ / 70 marks

Mixed questions

1. Underline **two noun phrases** in each sentence below.

   a) The new library books are on the top shelf.

   b) Some helpful children have tidied the messy art area.

   c) The little kitten in the corner is drinking milk from a saucer.

   d) A roaring fire warmed us from the bitterly cold wind.

   4 marks

2. Rewrite the sentences below in the **passive voice**.

   a) A reliable bus driver drove us to our destination.

   _____

   b) The children in Year 6 have picked up the litter in the playground.

   _____

   c) A famous sculptor designed the statue.

   _____

   d) My uncle's best friend recommended him for the job.

   _____

   4 marks

3. Complete each sentence using the underlined words in the **present perfect tense**.

   a) Mum <u>sews</u> _____ her ripped T-shirt.

   b) Some children in my class <u>go</u> _____ on a school trip.

   2 marks

4. Rewrite the sentences below so that they are in **Standard English**.

   a) They have ate their breakfast.

   _____

   _____

   b) Rory seen his friends last night.

   _____

   _____

2 marks

5. Tick one box on each row to show the **tense** of the underlined verbs in each sentence.

Sentence	Present perfect	Past perfect	Present progressive	Past progressive
Mark <u>has shown</u> great determination in overcoming his recent illness.				
Sarena <u>is helping</u> Elise with her history homework.				
I told Mum I <u>had tidied</u> my bedroom, but it wasn't true.				
We <u>were watching</u> TV when you called.				

4 marks

6. Underline the **two words** in the passage below that are **synonyms**.

The fragile wings of the butterfly caught my immediate attention. I grabbed my camera, focused the lens and captured the beautiful creature as it landed on a flower.

1 mark

7. In which sentence could you leave out the **relative pronoun?**

Tick **one**.

Joe, whose dad works abroad, speaks to him on a video call at weekends. ☐

The dog which you like best has won the best breed competition. ☐

The party where I met Louie had a clown and a magician. ☐

1 mark

8. Insert **two apostrophes** to show contractions in each sentence below.

a) Henrys been showing off again but as hes so funny we just laugh.

b) If only youd told me you were coming, Id have made your favourite cake.

c) Itll be rubbish if we cant go swimming at the weekend.

d) Ive had better test results since Mr Smiths been my teacher.

8 marks

9. Rewrite the sentences below in the **active voice.**

a) We were shown to our seats by the cabin crew.

_____

b) The safety procedures were explained to us by the cabin manager.

_____

2 marks

10. Insert a **hyphen** in each sentence so that it contains a compound word acting as an adjective.

a) Martha is a gentle, kind hearted girl who loves animals.

b) Ethan, who is fair haired with brown eyes, takes after his dad.

c) Mum bought a high quality sound system for the kitchen.

d) Grandpa likes a low sugar biscuit with his cup of tea.

4 marks

11. Choose either '-ence' or '-ance' to change these verbs into **nouns**.

obey   _____   confide   _____

comply   _____   signify   _____

4 marks

12. Rewrite the following sentence in the **passive voice**.

Mr Hegarty won the vegetable competition at this year's village fair.

_____

_____

1 mark

13. Underline the **two words** in the sentence below that are **antonyms**.

Meg was certain she would commit to the holiday, despite a rather dubious report about the hotel.

1 mark

14. Complete the passage below after changing the words in the box into **nouns**.

resist   insure

After checking his _____ policy, Dad's _____
to claiming for the damage to his car vanished.

2 marks

15. Add the **suffix** '-cious' or '-tious', '-cial' or '-tial' to change each noun into an adjective.

Noun	Adjective	Noun	Adjective
caution		benefit	
nutrition		torrent	
grace		commerce	
face		suspect	

8 marks

16. Underline the word in the passage below that uses an **apostrophe** in a **contraction**.

It's going to be raining all day so we are going to Huw's.

1 mark

91

17. Which sentence below uses a **colon** correctly? Tick **one**.

Tarek had seen the girls before one was Mo's sister and: the other was his cousin. ☐

Tarek had seen the girls before: one was Mo's sister and the other was his cousin. ☐

Tarek had seen the girls: before one was Mo's sister and the other was his cousin. ☐

Tarek had seen the girls before one: was Mo's sister and the other was his cousin. ☐

☐ 1 mark

18. Choose either '-ible' or '-able' to change these verbs into **adjectives**.

believe _____   depend _____

flex _____   sense _____

☐ 4 marks

19. Which sentence below uses a **dash** correctly?

Tick **one**.

Dad was convinced – he'd won the lottery Mum wasn't so sure. ☐

Dad was convinced he'd won the lottery Mum wasn't – so sure. ☐

Dad was convinced he'd won the lottery – Mum wasn't so sure. ☐

Dad was convinced he'd won – the lottery Mum wasn't so sure. ☐

☐ 1 mark

20. Insert the missing apostrophe to show possession in each sentence below.

a) I found Lillys school bag behind the radiator in the cloakroom.

b) The sound of the horses hooves as they neared the finish line was deafening.

c) The girls hats are in the back of the car.

d) Parisa sewed a button on to Chriss shirt.

☐ 4 marks

21. Underline all the **determiners** in the passage below.

On the farm, we saw some chickens, lots of cows and two horses. The farmer let me try milking a cow, which was good fun until I fell off the stool. It only had three legs so perhaps that is why.

8 marks

22. Write **D** or **H** in each box to indicate whether each arrow is pointing to a **dash** or a **hyphen**.

Sean likes up-to-date fashion – he's a real trendsetter.

3 marks

23. Underline **two prepositions** in each sentence below.

a) Ivan worked in the garden all morning, then stopped for lunch.

b) I signed my name at the bottom of the page.

c) 'Have you ever been to my Gran's house by the sea?'

6 marks

24. Tick a box in each row to show whether each sentence contains a **relative pronoun**, a **coordinating conjunction** or a **subordinating conjunction**.

Sentence	Relative pronoun	Coordinating conjunction	Subordinating conjunction
Unless you behave yourself, you are not going out to play.			
I always have butter and jam on my toast in the morning.			
The leisure centre where I learnt to swim has shut down.			

3 marks

25. Rewrite the statement below so that it is a **question**.

Craig has always loved wild animals.

_____

1 mark

26. Underline the **relative clause** in each sentence below.

   a) We visited our former neighbours who moved to the coast last year.

   b) Last year, when I had just turned seven, Mum passed her driving test.

   c) My dog Travis, whose bark is very loud, is actually a 'gentle giant'.

   3 marks

27. **What is the function of the sentence below?**

   What a terrible mess you have made of the kitchen

   Tick **one**.

   statement ☐

   exclamation ☐

   question ☐

   command ☐

   1 mark

28. **Complete each sentence by writing the verbs in brackets in the past perfect tense.**

   a) Elaya (see) _____ the present under the tree and was sure it was hers!

   b) The bird (fly) _____ from the nest to search for food for its chicks.

   c) It was only after she (leave) _____ the shop that Elise remembered her purse was still on the counter.

   d) Mum (forget) _____ that it was her sister's birthday, so she raced out to buy a present.

   4 marks

29. **Which sentence below is in the passive voice?**

   Tick **one**.

   My sick dog was examined by the caring vet. ☐

   I sat by the lake and painted the scene. ☐

   Paula said it was time to leave. ☐

   Sam rushed to get home before it was dark. ☐

   1 mark

30. Underline **two adjectives** in each sentence below.

   a) My black umbrella is very scruffy.

   b) Will was bored with his new video game already.

   c) Choppy seas and gale-force winds meant the boat could not set sail.

   d) Lin-Lee decided her new shoes looked odd.

8 marks

31. Label each box to show the **word class** of each word indicated by an arrow.

A	B	C	D	E	F
noun	verb	adjective	adverb	preposition	pronoun

Eventually, they found the entrance to a hidden cave and decided to explore it.

6 marks

32. Underline the **determiners** in each sentence below.

   a) Maria put some glue on the back of the paper.

   b) Please take those chocolate brownies out of the oven and cut them into several pieces.

2 marks

33. Write a sentence using the word <u>bite</u> as a **verb.**

_____

   Write a sentence using the word <u>bite</u> as a **noun.**

_____

2 marks

34. Complete the sentence by inserting a suitable **adverb.**

   Christie trains _____ so it is little wonder he is player of the match again.

1 mark

35. **What is the word class of the underlined word in the sentence below?**

My dog is a Labrador. What's yours?

Tick **one**.

a determiner ☐

a possessive determiner ☐

a possessive pronoun ☐

an adverbial ☐

1 mark

36. **Rewrite the sentence below so that it starts with the adverbial.**

The children and their parents arrived for parents' evening at 7 o'clock sharp.

_____

2 marks

37. **What is the word class of each underlined word?**

Dad likes to garden when he is off work. _____

Dad likes to work in the garden when he
is off work. _____

2 marks

38. **Underline the object in each sentence below.**

a) A huge shark was found in the shallow waters.

b) Do you still have that car with the retractable roof?

c) Bertie dropped her pencil on the floor.

d) We waited for the saline solution to evaporate.

4 marks

39. **Underline three prepositions in the sentence below.**

A mouse ran across the kitchen floor and into a hole in the wall.

3 marks

40. **Draw lines to match each prefix with a word on the right.**

in	respective
de	trustful
il	considerate
dis	logical
ir	construct

5 marks

41. Find **one word** in each sentence below that is missing its **silent letter**. Rewrite the word correctly on the line on the right. You might need a dictionary to help you.

a) We had samon for dinner, followed by a delicious dessert. _____

b) It is doutful whether our team will win the championship. _____

c) The thisle is the national flower of Scotland. _____

d) Leo helps on the farm during laming season. _____

4 marks

42. Underline the **three verbs** in the sentence below.

The horses raced towards the finish line as the crowd screamed and applauded.

3 marks

43. Insert the missing **inverted commas** in the sentence below.

I'd like to introduce you to your new teacher, said Mr McDermott.

2 marks

44. Rewrite the sentence below so that it starts with the **subordinate clause**.

I love cross-country running even though I'm not as fast as most of my friends.

_____

2 marks

45. Insert the missing punctuation to show the words in **parenthesis** in the sentence below.

Mum has lived in England a long time twenty-five years to be exact but she still misses her childhood home.

1 mark

Total: [   ] / 138 marks

Answers

Page 5
Challenge 1
1. a) He switched his <u>computer</u> on and sat down at his <u>desk</u>.
   b) I hurt my <u>knee</u> during the <u>match</u>.
   c) Black <u>ice</u> can make <u>footpaths</u> very dangerous to walk on.
   d) <u>Penguins</u> have <u>flippers</u> to help them swim.

Challenge 2
1. In the summer term, our teacher read us a book called The Hobbit. ✓
2. As we listened to the incredible <u>music</u>, we felt the <u>passion</u> of the talented <u>musicians</u>.

Challenge 3
1.

Common nouns	Abstract nouns
giraffe	disgrace
paint	pleasure
screen	disappointment
insect	mystery
bubble	rage
feather	mood

2. Last Thursday, we took the bus to Nottingham for our weekly swimming lesson.

Page 7
Challenge 1
1. a) The children are going home now after a <u>long</u>, <u>hard</u> day of tests and revision.
   b) Ravi is <u>bored</u> as it hasn't stopped raining and he wants to play football with his <u>best</u> friend.
   c) Dad likes to wear his <u>stripy</u> shirt when he goes to a <u>fancy</u> restaurant with Mum.
   d) The <u>blue</u> whale, weighing approximately 150 tons, is the <u>largest</u> animal on Earth.

Challenge 2
1. a) Thick snow lay on <u>the fields around the farmhouse</u>.
   b) The jubilant crowd cheered as the players received <u>the huge, silver cup adorned with ribbons</u>.
   c) We arrived at the big house and looked at <u>the wooden door with its enormous brass handle</u>.
   d) Our Christmas tree is decorated with <u>a variety of glittery gold and silver baubles</u>.
2. Award up to 2 marks for a suitable sentence, punctuated correctly, containing a noun phrase.

Challenge 3
1. a) Orla is **hungrier** than Jack.
   b) Rory's story is **more interesting** than mine.
   c) Dan's fancy-dress costume is the **most impressive** of them all.
2. Award **1 mark** for each sentence that includes an expanded noun phrase, e.g:
   the grey mountains topped with snow
   the inky black, velvet sky with twinkling stars

Page 9
Challenge 1
1. Award 1 mark, up to a maximum of 10, for each verb underlined.
   a) We <u>ran</u> to the shop and <u>ordered</u> vanilla and chocolate ice-creams.
   b) The rain <u>lashes</u> against the window as we <u>stare</u> out of the classroom window.
   c) Bethan usually <u>eats</u> her sandwiches with Bill but today he <u>is</u> absent.
   d) Mum <u>wants</u> a new car; unfortunately, she <u>hasn't</u> enough money.
   e) My dog, Monty, <u>is</u> a loyal companion who <u>has</u> a calm and friendly temperament.

Challenge 2
1. a) The farmer <u>carefully</u> placed the new-born chicks in the hay.
   b) I'm going home <u>early</u> today as I have a dentist appointment.
   c) Our teacher <u>occasionally</u> lets us go on an early break.
   d) Harry's cousin has <u>never</u> been to a firework display.
2. Accept any suitable adverb, spelt correctly, e.g:
   After her run, Ella drank **thirstily** from the water fountain.

Challenge 3
1. J K Rowling's new book is <u>quite</u> good, but I much prefer her last one.
2. Mum answered the phone <u>rather</u> sleepily as she had slept in.
3. Today's maths test was very <u>hard</u>.   **adjective**
   Jon worked <u>hard</u> in today's maths test.   **adverb**
4. Award up to 2 marks for a suitable sentence that has been punctuated correctly and where the word 'fast' is used as an adverb, e.g:
   Daniel runs **fast** but his little sister is the best runner in the school.

Page 11
Challenge 1
1. a) Our school was presented with the football league cup <u>last week</u>.
   b) We have won <u>every year</u> since I've been playing.
   c) As I am the team captain, I <u>politely</u> shook hands with the head teacher.
   d) A photographer took our picture and everyone cheered <u>excitedly</u>.

Challenge 2
1. Award 1 mark per sentence for the fronted adverbial correctly placed and followed by a comma.
   a) With no time to lose, we reached the platform.

b) From the top of the summit, they could see for miles.

c) Energetically, Gretchen brushed the kitchen floor.

d) For her special birthday, Fiona was given a new laptop.

Challenge 3

1. Award up to 2 marks for a suitable sentence starting with a fronted adverbial followed by a comma, and an initial capital letter and final full stop, e.g: Last weekend, we went for a long hike in the hills.

2. Accept suitable adverbials, e.g: We ate our picnic **beside the river. After a while**, Bella said she wanted to play cricket. The sun blazed **furiously**, so we set our game up in the shade. It was growing dark when we left **in the evening**.

Page 13
Challenge 1

1. It – **the gloomy distance;** them – **Fred and Eli**

2. Award **1 mark** for each pronoun underlined.

   a) <u>She</u> let <u>me</u> share the book.

   b) Please tell <u>me</u> what time <u>it</u> is.

   c) <u>We</u> saw <u>them</u> in the park yesterday.

   d) <u>They</u> said <u>it</u> was an old castle.

Challenge 2

1. We decided that Bavini and **I** should tell the teacher our good news.
   Dad cooked Frankie and **me** a lovely lunch on Saturday.

2. Erin visited the castle with her mum and dad. **They** told her **it** was haunted.

Challenge 3

1. I gave them their books back but they didn't give me mine. ✓

2. That bike isn't **yours. Yours** is over there!

Page 15
Challenge 1

1. Award 1 mark for each underlined **determiner**.

   a) After Dad found <u>a</u> film we all wanted to watch on <u>the</u> TV, he handed out <u>some</u> chocolate brownies.

   b) <u>Those</u> children have been accused of dropping <u>lots of</u> litter in <u>the</u> playground.

   c) <u>Two</u> field mice appeared in <u>the</u> farmer's kitchen after <u>the</u> wheat was harvested.

   d) <u>Each</u> apple we took from <u>the</u> tree was crunchy, crisp and cool, and we savoured <u>every</u> bite.

Challenge 2

1. **a)** Harry did **his** homework, then packed **his** schoolbag ready for the morning.

   b) **Example: My** teacher is leaving to travel the world with **her** husband.

   c) **Example:** Ella said **their** dog had been missing since she came back from **her** piano lesson.

   d) I think **my** handwriting has improved since I've started holding **my** pencil differently.

Challenge 3
1. **Answers will vary. Example:**
   Many children eat **lots of** fruit. Personally, I eat **five** portions **every** day. I also like to do **some** exercise on **a** daily basis. There is **no** doubt that I feel and look healthier after **several** months of following **this** routine.

Page 17
Challenge 1

1. Award one mark for each preposition underlined.

   a) Valerie took the bus <u>into</u> town and met Juliette <u>at</u> the shops.

   b) I put my dish <u>of</u> ice-cream <u>on</u> the table.

   c) Freddie goes <u>to</u> his swimming lesson <u>at</u> 3 o'clock.

   d) The children walked <u>across</u> the bridge and sat <u>beside</u> the river.

Challenge 2

1. **Answers will vary. Example:**
   Go <u>through</u> the front door, go <u>up</u> the stairs, turn right, go <u>along</u> the corridor then turn left <u>into</u> my bedroom.

2. **Answers will vary. Example:** Anya sat **next to** me **on** the bus when we went **on** our school trip **to** the Lake District. We arrived **at** 11 o'clock and had our lunch **at** some picnic tables **beside** the river.

Challenge 3

1.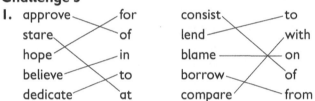

Page 19
Challenge 1

1. **a)** <u>Brea</u> helps her mum in the kitchen.

   b) <u>She</u> usually clears the table after meals.

   c) <u>Her dad</u> will then wash the dishes.

   d) Then <u>they</u> all sit down to watch TV.

Challenge 2

1. Flooding is causing damage to homes in this region. ✓

2. The number of children arriving late **is** increasing.
   The good news **is** that we can go home early today.
   The ladies' changing rooms **are** closed today.

Challenge 3
Answers will vary. Examples:

1. **The choir** sang **their songs** beautifully.

2. **Some children** have been dropping **litter** in the corridor.

3. **Mr Smith** enjoys baking **cakes**, which he brings to school.

Pages 20–23
Progress test 1

1. **a)** My <u>new</u> computer is really <u>fast.</u>

   b) After the <u>heavy</u> rainfall, we discovered a <u>small</u> leak in our attic.

- **c)** Becky felt <u>miserable</u> when she realised she had upset her <u>best</u> friend.
- **d)** I am <u>impatient</u> to receive a <u>long</u> letter from my cousin in Spain.
2. a noun phrase ✓
3. Award 1 mark for each verb underlined.
   - **a)** The bakery <u>sells</u> such tasty pies that I <u>decided</u> to <u>have</u> two.
   - **b)** When Ezra <u>woke</u>, he <u>remembered</u> his terrible dream and <u>panicked</u>.
   - **c)** The hotel guests <u>packed</u>, <u>paid</u> their bill and <u>left</u>.
   - **d)** Will <u>wants</u> to <u>learn</u> Spanish but he <u>finds</u> languages difficult.
4. Just last week, Chen mastered all his times tables. ✓
5. a noun. ✓
6. Unfortunately, when we reached the summit, it was

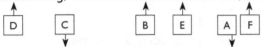

covered with a dense mist which ruined our view.
7. **a)** Sophie usually eats <u>a</u> slice of toast for breakfast but today she had <u>some</u> cereal.
   - **b)** <u>The</u> soldiers marched towards <u>the</u> barracks, looking forward to <u>a</u> well-deserved rest.
   - **c)** Jenni has <u>two</u> younger sisters and <u>an</u> older brother.
   - **d)** We took <u>the</u> late train to Scotland and Gran met us on <u>the</u> platform.
8. **Answers will vary. Example:**
   Dad likes to **hike** in the summer months as he hates cold weather.
   Dad took us on a **hike** in the summer.
9. **Award one mark per expanded noun phrase, up to a maximum of 2, for each sentence. Example:**
   Aaron and his little puppy with the big ears were playing in **the farmer's fields**.
   The little sail boat was tossed about on **enormous waves in the choppy ocean**.
10. Maria and Josef walked to the bus stop. **They** were late yet again and the bus had already left. Unlike **them**, **it** was always punctual. **They** went back home to tell their mum. **She** was cross but agreed to take **them** to school in her car. However, **it** wouldn't start as **she** had left her lights on, which meant **it** now had a flat battery.
11. **Answers will vary. Example:**
    Asqa stirred the mixture **thoroughly**, then put it into the cake tin.
12. a possessive pronoun ✓
13. **Award up to 2 marks for the adverbial correctly placed and followed by a comma.**
    After a long wait, we were relieved to get on the ferry.
14. Christian and Flo <u>care</u> deeply about their sick dog.
    verb
    Christian and Flo take good <u>care</u> of their sick dog.
    noun

15. **a)** Today, we baked <u>cakes</u> in school.
    - **b)** The dog is eating <u>a bone</u> at the bottom of the garden.
    - **c)** I dropped <u>a glass</u> on the kitchen floor.
    - **d)** The ranger rescued <u>the elephant</u> from the trap
16. I intended <u>to</u> sit <u>beside</u> James, but he wouldn't move <u>over</u>.
17. Xavier has <u>nearly</u> finished his art project. ✓
18. a pronoun ✓

Page 25
Challenge 1
1. **a)** It's time to go home.
   - **b)** Whose coat is this?
   - **c)** Are you coming with me?
   - **d)** We'll be late for the bus.
2. **Answers will vary. Examples:** I am eleven years old with dark, curly hair and brown eyes.
Challenge 2
1. **Example:** There was a crowd of people watching the firework display in the farmer's field.
2. Has Michael started revising for his test?
Challenge 3
1. **Answers will vary. Examples:**
   Question: Where are you going on holiday this year?
   Question: What is your favourite book?

Page 27
Challenge 1
1. **a)** Please <u>help</u> me tidy up the kitchen.
   - **b)** <u>Bring</u> the dog inside please; it's raining!
   - **c)** Carefully <u>mix</u> the butter, sugar and eggs.
   - **d)** <u>Hurry up</u> please – I don't want to miss the start of the show.
Challenge 2
1. What a dreadful night of wind and rain that was ✓
2. **Answers will vary. Example:**
   - **a)** **Finish** your breakfast quickly!
   - **b)** **Look** both ways before you cross the road.
Challenge 3
1. **Answers will vary. Example:**
   Please brush your teeth before you go to bed.
2. **Answers will vary. Example:**
   How fantastic your painting is!
3. How many people were affected by the storm. ✓

Page 29
Challenge 1
1. Ushma has a dog **but** she hasn't got a cat.
2. Gran told my brother **and** me we could either read a book **or** watch a film, **but** then we would have to go to bed.
3. Dev played football <u>until</u> it started raining.
   The criminals were soon caught <u>as</u> they had been careless.

Challenge 2

1.

Sentence	Main clause	Subordinate clause
After we had been swimming, <u>we went to the new restaurant for a pizza</u>.	✓	
Nick was passionate about football <u>even though he'd never been to a big match</u>.		✓
<u>We managed to make it to school</u> once the icy roads had been gritted.	✓	
Katie said we should meet in the park <u>before we started our sponsored run</u>.		✓

Challenge 3

1. Answers will vary. Example:
We started to pack up as the sun began to set.

2. Award up to 2 marks if subordinate clause is correctly placed and followed by a comma.
If the weather stays fine, we are going abseiling at the weekend.

Page 31
Challenge 1

1. a) My cousin <u>who lives in Scotland</u> is coming for Christmas.

b) My great-grandfather was born in 1939, <u>when World War II started</u>.

Challenge 2

1. a) The weather, **which** has been rather grim, has thankfully perked up.

b) The day **when/that** my baby brother was born was the best day ever!

c) Muir's best friend, **who** is moving house, is planning a party.

d) The shop on the corner, **where** the traffic lights are, is new.

Challenge 3

1. The toothache I had last night has finally eased. The year we won the World Cup was amazing!

2. The book that I read last year has been made into a film. ✓

Page 33
Challenge 1

1. Everyone in our class **liked** our new teacher, Mrs Semple. She always **helped** and **encouraged** us. Her motto **was** 'dare to dream!'

Challenge 2

1. The doctor assisted the injured player when she limped off the pitch. ✓

2. Answers will vary. Accept any suitable verb as follows: a) simple past tense; b) simple present tense. Examples:

a) This year, we are going to London to stay with our cousins but last year they **came** to us.

b) Mum is always telling us not to leave lights on but she often **forgets** to switch them off herself!

Challenge 3

1. Mollie **took** great care when she **drew** the map. Sol **ran** over the finish line and **threw** himself on the ground in relief.

2. catch – **caught**; do – **did**; drive – **drove**; buy – **bought**; fight – **fought**; fly – **flew**

Page 35
Challenge 1

1. a) Michael <u>has made</u> the decision to train for the London Marathon.

b) There is a lot of snow so Mum and Dad <u>have decided</u> to take us sledging.

2. a) Georgie <u>had written</u> a diary regularly for years, then suddenly she stopped.

b) Nikolas went to the dentist as he <u>had suffered</u> with toothache for weeks.

Challenge 2

1. a) Dad **has taken** the ferry to France to see his cousin.

b) I **have eaten** a large portion of fish and chips.

c) Farida **has done** a lot of fundraising for charity.

d) We **have been** on holiday in Cornwall.

Challenge 3

1. Our neighbours still have chickens now. ✓

2. She hadn't realised that Henry VIII was so overweight! ✓

Page 37
Challenge 1

1. a) <u>I'm planning</u> my writing homework using a colour-coded mind map.

b) We have been thinking about moving to the coast but now Dad <u>is considering</u> other options.

c) You won't believe who <u>is moving</u> to our neighbourhood next month!

2. a) I thought I heard a loud bang but maybe I <u>was dreaming</u>.

b) As Mum <u>was painting</u> the kitchen, she noticed a damp patch had appeared on the ceiling.

c) Our uncles <u>were expecting</u> compensation after a car accident in which they broke their arms.

Challenge 2

1.

Sentence	Present perfect	Past perfect	Present progressive	Past progressive
Kasim is riding his bike to school this term.			✓	
I had thought he might prefer the bus.		✓		
He has tried cycling in the past.	✓			
However, he was finding it hard in the winter.				✓

Challenge 3

1. As Juan <u>was walking</u> to the leisure centre, he met Sonia. They <u>were chatting</u> for a while before they parted company. When Juan arrived, the fire alarm <u>was ringing</u>.

Page 39
Challenge 1

1.

Sentence	Active voice	Passive voice
Connie was standing by the door when she heard the bell ring.	✓	
Our dog was treated by the vet when he had kennel cough.		✓
Harry was announced the winner by the competition judge.		✓
Mum's temperamental car is usually repaired by Greg, a mechanic.	✓	

Challenge 2

1. a) <u>The anglers</u> caught 〈35kg of fish〉 over the course of the day.
   b) <u>My dog</u> chased 〈your cat〉 into the park.
2. a) <u>My grandad's temperature</u> was taken 〈by a nurse〉.
   b) <u>We</u> were advised 〈by the police to〉 install an alarm.
3. a) A nurse took my grandad's temperature.
   b) The police advised us to install an alarm.

Challenge 3

1. **Award up to 2 marks for the following:**
   We were checked in and shown to our rooms by the receptionist.
2. **Award up to 2 marks for the following:**
   We were checked in and shown to our rooms.

Page 41
Challenge 1

1. a) The other team <u>will</u> be hard to beat as they've been training hard.
   b) Freddy <u>can</u> play piano and guitar to a very high standard.
   c) Jess knows she <u>should</u> phone her grandparents more often.
   d) The teacher says we <u>can</u> have an extended playtime.

2.

Shows a degree of certainty	Shows an obligation	Shows ability	Shows permission
will	should	can	can

Challenge 2

1. a) I **can** / must speak two foreign languages because I've lived in Italy and France.
   b) Mum said Sal can / **must** have a sore throat as she has coughed all night.
   c) The teacher said we **could** / ought to play either hockey or golf, depending on the weather.
2. a) You should <u>probably</u> leave early today as it looks like it might snow.
   b) If you would only try a bit harder, <u>maybe</u> you'd succeed!

Challenge 3

1. **Answers may vary. Examples:**
   a) Taking exercise is **definitely** good for your health.
   b) Joe had **clearly** eaten his breakfast, judging by the amount of crumbs on the table.

Pages 42–45
Progress test 2

1. a) Dad <u>has built</u> an extension on the back of our house.
   b) Some thoughtless people <u>have dropped</u> litter in the woods.
   c) Mr Martin <u>has gone</u> to a teachers' conference.
   d) A swarm of bees <u>has flown</u> towards the hives.
2. a) <u>Bring</u> me your test papers, please, but first <u>check</u> you have written your name at the top.
   b) <u>Stick</u> a stamp on the envelope then <u>take</u> the letter to the post office please.
   c) <u>Turn</u> left at the end of the road, then <u>go</u> first right.
   d) Please <u>look</u> under the mat and <u>see</u> if you can find the spare key.
3. adverb
4. a) Maya **is watching** the Wimbledon tennis final with her mum.
   b) We **are painting** a picture of a bowl of fruit.
   c) Felipe **is hoping** his team gets at least a draw today.
   d) Mum **is brushing** the leaves up before she cuts the grass.
5. a) I enjoyed the book <u>although it was hard to understand the plot</u>.
   b) <u>As we knew it was going to be a long journey</u>, we packed a big lunch.
   c) Isabella wore her waterproof coat <u>even though it wasn't raining</u>.
   d) The children were told what to do <u>if the fire alarm started ringing</u>.
6. In science, we studied <u>the</u> different features of <u>some</u> minibeasts that we found under <u>a</u> plank.
7. **Award up to 2 marks for the adverbial placed correctly followed by a comma.**
   Before lunch, we finished our science experiment.
8. The car we bought a few years ago appears to have a fault with its engine.
9. The plumber has come to fix the tap.
   <u>The plumber</u> has promised to fix <u>the tap</u> within the hour. ↑ [He/She] ↑ [it]
10. a) I <u>was waiting</u> ages for the bus, which had been held up due to an accident.
    b) As we <u>were planning</u> our visit to the leisure centre, Mum got a call to say it was closed.
    c) Dad <u>was washing</u> the dishes when he smashed Mum's favourite glass.
    d) Although we didn't hear or see anything suspicious, our dog <u>was barking</u> all night.

11. a) Our fares were collected by the train conductor.
    b) The cat was rescued from the top of the tree by the fireman.
    c) Our old armchair was re-covered by an excellent local company.
    d) Our kitchen extension was planned by Mum.
12. a) A swarm of bees attacked us as we were eating our picnic. / As we were eating our picnic, a swarm of bees attacked us.
    b) Officials escorted the celebrity through the crowd.
13.

Sentence	Relative pronoun	Coordinating conjunction	Subordinating conjunction
Stanley is good in all subject areas, but he performs best in English.		✓	
Our teacher, whose dog recently had pups, showed us a video of them playing.	✓		
Although it's a sunny day, the wind is actually very cold.			✓

14. Has Enrico studied hard for his piano exam?
15. a) The cake <u>that I baked</u> is chocolate with a blackberry jam filling.
    b) We have just watched a comedy film, <u>which has really cheered us up</u>.
    c) Our vegetable patch, <u>where the garden slopes slightly downhill</u>, is thriving.
16. Sentence 1: Dragonflies at one point had been on Earth for 300 million years but aren't any longer.
    Sentence 2: Dragonflies have been on Earth for around 300 million years and are still here now.
17. a) Sian **had drawn** the curtains against the dark night when she heard a knock at the door.
    b) Ryan successfully reached the summit even though he **had lost** some time due to the snowstorm.
18. exclamation ✓

Page 47
Challenge 1
1. a) Alfie consulted the recipe book and noted that he would need sultanas, sugar, eggs, plain flour and cherries.
   b) We have seen a wide range of weather this week: sunshine, gales, hailstones, fog and blizzards.
   c) Mum has been planting seeds; she hopes to have home-grown aubergines, chillies, tomatoes, beetroot and carrots in the summer months.
   d) The skiers packed their thermal vests, hats, ski socks, gloves and scarves into their bags and rucksacks.

Challenge 2
1. In the second sentence, Bethan asks three people to help her. (In the first sentence, if there is no comma, 'Maggie Bailey' would be one person.)
2. Before school, I usually sit in the library with my book.
   During the summer, we went on a camping trip to Devon.

Challenge 3
1. **Award up to 2 marks for the subordinate clause correctly placed followed by a comma.**
   Even though they are in their seventies, my grandparents are excellent climbers.
2. After they left James, Zayn and Chris went to the park.
3. After they left, James, Zayn and Chris went to the park.

Page 49
Challenge 1
1. ‚I've just discovered that our cousins are coming for the weekend, said Brogan.

   ✓   ✓   ☐   ☐

2. 'I've just seen Bertie walking his new dog!' exclaimed Mia. ✓

Challenge 2
1. **Award 1 mark for each set of inverted commas positioned correctly up to a maximum of 2 marks.**
   a) 'How many items are on today's agenda?' asked the Year 6 House Captain.
   b) 'Please help me peel the carrots,' said Mum, 'otherwise dinner will be very late.'
2. 'I'll help you with your homework,' Sam told his sister. **Accept slight differences, e.g.** 'I'll help you with your homework,' Sam said to his sister.

Challenge 3
1. I've just read an article called 'Life in the Palace' about the Queen. One source said: 'Her Majesty is always in bed by 10pm.' Another said: 'Her Majesty likes cereal and toast for breakfast.' My favourite quote was by the palace dog trainer who revealed: 'Her Majesty likes to curl up with her dogs on the sofa while she watches a programme called 'Walkies' on TV.'

Page 51
Challenge 1
1.

Sentence	Contraction	Possession
My sister's making me a bowl of soup.	✓	
Our class's representative is Mariam.		✓
Ben was sure he'd brought his homework.	✓	
The police found the thieves' footsteps.		✓

Challenge 2

1. wasn't; I'd; we'll; they'd; should've; shan't; they're; won't

Challenge 3

1. The girls' books are overdue.
   The princess's crown is studded with diamonds and rubies.

2. **It's** with no small amount of fear that we creep through the forest, not wanting to wake the beast from **its** sleep. We know **it's** in **its** cave, but **it's** bound to hear us if we aren't careful. **It's** almost dark now so **it's** best we find shelter before **it's** too late.

Page 53

Challenge 1

1. My brother Miles (the one who's mad about music) is going to a concert tonight. ✓

Challenge 2

1. relative clause. ✓

Challenge 3

1. a) Following the match, we went home – tired and muddy – to a bowl of hot soup.
   b) Marco – tightrope walker extraordinaire – amazed the crowd with his daring agility.

2. **Accept pairs of brackets, commas or dashes. Examples:**
   a) Luckily, Dana (with only seconds to spare) managed to get the last train home.
   b) We cheered when the trapeze artists – with extraordinary agility – swapped in mid-air.

Page 55

Challenge 1

1. Last time I visited, she made veggie burgers and salad; we sat outside and talked until the sun went down. ✓

Challenge 2

1. a) We need to pack the following for our trip to the seaside: swimming costumes, goggles, snorkels, masks and flippers.
   b) The Head Teacher made her last announcement of the evening: tea and coffee would be served in the staffroom.
   c) For our art lesson today, we will need a range of equipment: scissors, glue, paper, paints and water.
   d) There was clearly only one thing to do: report the incident to the police and let them take action.

Challenge 3

1. My favourite books are the following: 'Harry Potter and the Philosopher's Stone' and 'Harry Potter and the Goblet of Fire', both by J K Rowling; 'Absolutely Everything' by Christopher Lloyd, which is great for dipping into; and 'The Boy at the Back of the Class' by Anjari Rauf. 'A Boy Called Hope' by Lara Williamson is an interesting read about family relationships and friendships; I should have finished it by next week.

Page 57

Challenge 1

1. a) We had reached the mountain's summit – or had we?
   b) There was only one thing for it – sink or swim.
   c) 'I wanted *Sami* to come swimming with me – not *you*!' moaned Freddie.
   d) The maths paper was very hard – so hard that I think I've failed.

Challenge 2

1. a) Auntie Sal only drinks sugar-free cola and lemonade.
   b) Vadim has been a hard-working man all his life.
   c) After the argument and a soul-searching evening, Clara realised she'd been wrong.

Challenge 3

1. 'It can't be – it is – yes, it's really you!' exclaimed Jamil when he opened the front door.

2. **re-signed** means the lawyer signed the paperwork again.
   resigned means the lawyer handed in his notice/ quit his job.

Page 59

Challenge 1

1.

Genre	Formal	Informal
A text to your friend		✓
A letter to the local council	✓	
A postcard to a cousin		✓
Your diary entry		✓
A speech for a debate in which you are participating	✓	
An email to a sibling		✓

Challenge 2

1. **Answers may vary. Examples:**
   a) We aren't going to the park – we've got visitors.
   b) Pick those shoes up or I'll be very cross.
   c) Hayley would have helped you if you'd asked her.

Challenge 3

1. Hear you've been a bit unwell lately. Such a shame but hopefully you're a bit better now. <u>If this is not the case, a doctor ought to be contacted</u>. Send me a quick text to let me know how you're doing.

2. were ✓

Pages 60–63

Progress test 3

1. Our history teacher said we would be exploring the lives of Catherine of Aragon, Anne Boleyn, Jane Seymour, Anne of Cleves, Catherine Howard and Catherine Parr.

2. Although the forecast isn't great, we're really looking forward to the school fair.

3. Our cousin's coming to join us so that'll be fun. ✓
4. a) Mum **has looked** everywhere for her keys.
   b) Some children **have left** their PE kit in school.
   c) Miles **has gone** to a concert.
   d) James **has thrown** the ball to Cerys.
5. a) In future, you really should check you've brought your PE kit with you.
   b) Every afternoon, our teacher reads to us from our class novel.
6. **Accept a pair of brackets, dashes or commas. Example:**
   We went white-water rafting – an often dangerous sport – and thoroughly enjoyed ourselves.
7. <u>My cousin Jack</u> lives in ⟨a cottage⟩ next to the sea.
8. a) I had reached the end of my magical adventure – or so I thought.
   b) I turned the corner and surveyed the scene – a horror that words could not describe!
9. **Answers will vary. Examples:**
   I was asked to represent our school at the debating competition. As Bill is absent, the head teacher will re-present his prize another time.
10. a) The judge's decision was final; Sarena was undoubtedly the clear winner.
    b) When we go hiking, we take a flask of coffee; it warms us up in the winter months.
11. Dad's car may be <u>ancient</u> but it is <u>reliable</u>, and gets us where we need to go.
12.

Sentence	Present perfect	Past perfect	Present progressive	Past progressive
Phillip <u>has decided</u> to buy a new house after much consideration.	✓			
Sammie is <u>studying</u> the works of a famous artist.			✓	
I was sure that I <u>had handed</u> my homework in.		✓		
You <u>were sleeping</u> when I phoned you.				✓

13. a) We were at the cinema when we saw a flashing light.
    b) It could have been a police car or an ambulance.
    c) We weren't worried but hoped it wasn't anything serious.
    d) When we came out, we didn't see anything odd.
14. a) Maria is a sensible, quick-thinking girl who can be trusted at all times.
    b) My little brother may be forgetful, annoying and accident-prone but he has a heart of gold.
    c) On the long journey to Grandma's, Dad called into a self-service café so we could have a snack.
    d) Verity is very bad-tempered in the mornings but by lunchtime she is laughing and joking.
15. I think it's going to rain. While we're waiting for better weather, why don't we go to <u>Mo's</u> ?
16. a) We have just been to <u>the</u> theatre to see <u>a</u> really great show.

b) There were <u>some</u> great performances and <u>two</u> amazing singers!
17. We clambered to the top and fell into each other's arms – now we could celebrate! ✓
18. 'Please place your test papers on my desk and line up quietly for lunch,' said the teacher.
19. a) After many days of searching, **Millie's** PE kit was eventually found in the lost-property cupboard.
    b) As I neared my **journey's** end, I felt excited about seeing my family and friends again.
    c) Our two **cats'** beds are in the corner of the utility room, next to the boiler.
    d) The **princesses'** gowns were kept in glass wardrobes in each of their bedrooms.
20. Auntie Freida likes low-fat yoghurt – she's watching her weight.
    [H]   [D]
21. a) Monty buried his bone <u>in</u> the garden then two minutes later dug it <u>up</u> again.
    b) Finley usually sits <u>beside</u> Katie <u>at</u> the front table.

Page 65
Challenge 1
1. **Answers will vary. Examples:**

Adjective	Antonym
weak	strong
messy	tidy
energetic	lifeless
bright	dull
extrovert	introvert

Challenge 2
1. **Answers will vary. Examples:**
   enticing; eager
2. **Answers will vary. Example:** dismantled
3. **dis**regard; **im**proper; **in**audible
Challenge 3
1. industrious, hard-working
2. disadvantage, benefit

Page 67
Challenge 1
1. in—— responsible
   mis—— ability
   il—— respectful
   dis—— logical
   ir—— inform**Challenge 2**

1.

Root word	Word with prefix	Definition of word with prefix
cover	**re**cover	*To get well again*
cover	**dis**cover	**To find something out**
appear	**dis**appear	*To go missing*
appear	**re**appear	**To appear again**
graph	**auto**graph	*A person's signature*
pilot	**auto**pilot	**When machinery moves automatically, without human involvement**

Challenge 3
a) semi – **half** b) sub – **under/below**
c) uni – **one/single** d) mono – **one/single**

Page 69
Challenge 1
1.

Noun	Adjective	Noun	Adjective
malice	**malicious**	repetition	**repetitious**
ambition	**ambitious**	space	**spacious**
nutrition	**nutritious**	vice	**vicious**

Challenge 2
1.

Noun	Adjective	Noun	Adjective
president	**presidential**	face	**facial**
finance	**financial**	confidence	**confidential**
torrent	**torrential**	essence	**essential**

Challenge 3
1. suspicious; fictitious; delicious
2. a) Our school policy is that only **nutritious** food should be served.
   b) Mum's charity work has been very **influential** in raising awareness of the homeless.
   c) On our way to the shops, we saw a **suspicious** character lurking on the corner.
   d) The rumours that our teacher was retiring proved to be entirely **fictitious**.

Page 71
Challenge 1
1. tolerance; hesitance; dominance; observance; appliance; obedience

Challenge 2
1.

Verb	Adjective	Noun
differ	**different**	**difference**
resist	**resistant**	**resistance**
reside	**resident/residential**	**residence/resident**
insist	**insistent**	**insistence**
buoy	**buoyant**	**buoyancy**

Challenge 3
1. a) Our trek in the Peak District was a real **endurance** test!
   b) The **defendant** refused to admit her guilt at the trial.
   c) After much **reassurance** from my friends, I confronted the bully in the playground.
   d) Stella's **reliance** on her brother for help with her homework has got to stop.
2. Change the 'y' to 'i' before adding the suffix: **reliance** and **compliance**

Page 73
Challenge 1
1.

	Adjective	Adverb
adore	adorable	adorably
prefer	preferable	preferably
desire	desirable	desirably
accept	acceptable	acceptably

Challenge 2
1. a) Dad gets **irritable** if we leave a mess in the kitchen.
   b) Our teacher gives us a **reasonable** amount of homework.
   c) In the autumn, it is **advisable** to carry an umbrella.
   d) Our caravan site is only **accessible** from the coast road.
   e) Last summer, the weather in Wales was truly **terrible**.

Challenge 3
1. a) We have a new, much more **fashionable** / fashionible summer uniform.
   b) After the kitchen fire, our house was **uninhabitable** / unhabitible.
   c) Although Gwen isn't very flexable / **flexible**, she enjoys her yoga classes.
   d) When I am eighteen, I'll be **eligible** / eligable to vote in the election.
2. justifiably; noticeably; reliably; changeably

Page 75
Challenge 1
1. a) **transferred** b) **preference**
   c) **conferred** d) **reference**

Challenge 2
1. a) I inferred from the text that the character had something to hide.
   b) Sam didn't realise that the teacher was referring to his art work.
   c) The decision has been deferred until the end of the year.
   d) My favourite player is transferring to another club.

Challenge 3
1. a) Dad produced what Mum called 'a burnt **offering**' from the oven.
   b) Henry's uncle is a firm but fair football **referee**.
   c) Our head teacher is attending an educational **conference**.
   d) Molly's painting of the scene **differs/differed** from Rav's.

Page 77
Challenge 1
1.

'ough' pronounced 'uff'	'ough' pronounced 'oo'	'ough' pronounced 'oh'
enough tough	through	dough although
'ough' pronounced 'aw'	**'ough' pronounced 'ow'**	**'ough' pronounced 'o'**
brought ought thought fought bought	bough plough	trough

Challenge 2

1. brought, cough, thought, rough, tough, ought, bough

Challenge 3

1. a) The cattle drink from a **trough** when they are thirsty.
   b) Dad stretched the pizza **dough** before putting it on an oven tray.
   c) The old farmer prefers an old-fashioned horse-drawn **plough** to modern-day machinery.

Page 79

Challenge 1

1. **Also accept 'either' in column 'ei' with an 'ih' sound or column 'ei' with an 'ee' sound.**

'ei' after 'c' with an 'ee' sound	'ei' with an 'ee' sound	'ei' with an 'ay' sound	'ei' with an 'ih' sound	'ei' with an 'i' sound
perceive	protein	vein	foreign	height
deceit	caffeine	freight	forfeit	either

Challenge 2

1. Neither, Ancient, seized, fields, believe, neighbour's, fierce, shrieked, received, brief

Challenge 3

1. a) | n | i | e | c | e |
   b) | r | e | c | e | i | p | t |
   c) | b | e | i | g | e |
   d) | c | a | f | f | e | i | n | e |

Page 81

Challenge 1

1. h<u>our</u>; sole<u>mn</u>; <u>k</u>nit; s<u>w</u>ord; mus<u>c</u>le; <u>g</u>nome
2. sil<u>h</u>ouette, <u>p</u>neumonia, <u>p</u>sychology, hym<u>n</u>

Challenge 2

1. a) jostling   b) succumbed   c) gnarled

Challenge 3

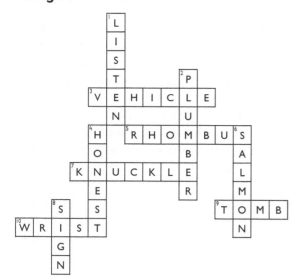

Page 83

Challenge 1

1. a) I saw a lovely **pair** / pear of shoes as I **passed** / past the shoe shop.
   b) George had to **pause** / paws the video as he couldn't **bear** / bare to watch the fighting.
   c) As the queen approached the 60th year of her rein / **reign**, the nation guest / **guessed** she would retire.
   d) We aren't aloud / **allowed** to waist / **waste** food as Mum is conscious of those who are starving.

Challenge 2

1. It was hard to except / **accept** that our family dog had snapped at our neighbour. I know you should always be weary / **wary** of any animal, but Monty has never been anything **except** / accept gentle and loving. Mum wanders / **wonders** if it might be something to do with the robotic **device** / devise our neighbour was using to cut his grass.

Challenge 3

1. due, proceeded, There, were, addition, weather, affected, descent, where, knew.

Pages 84–87

Progress test 4

1. assurance; innocence; frequency
2. a) Grace **had looked** everywhere for her homework diary.
   b) We **had thought** the film would be better than it turned out.
3. a) The trekkers had been planning their trip for many years; it was finally a reality.
   b) Gran is desperate for some company; we really must visit her this weekend.
4. obed**ience**; toler**ance**; confid**ence**; endur**ance**
5. **Answers will vary. Example:** The children were carefully supervised by the teachers as they climbed up the ropes.
6. Joseph's eyes lit up in <u>anticipation</u> of the weekend ahead. Although Mum had warned them all of the uncertain weather forecast, there was still an air of <u>expectancy</u> in the back of the car.
7. The children had done a <u>partial</u> clean of the classroom, in the knowledge that the cleaners would take a more <u>thorough</u> approach.
8. 'Your lack of **compliance** with our school rules is shocking!' scolded the teacher. 'I'd like your **assurance** that this behaviour won't happen again. Now, please have the **decency** to apologise to the teaching **assistant** who is upset.'
9.

Noun	Adjective	Noun	Adjective
part	**partial**	finance	**financial**
infection	**infectious**	president	**presidential**
vice	**vicious**	office	**official/officious**
space	**spacious/spatial**	influence	**influential**

10. I'm telling you now: the man over there in the corner is the lead singer of The Bramble Boys! ✓
11. hesit**ancy**; depend**ency**; vac**ancy**
12. unbeliev**ably**; horrible; incredibly; inaudible; remarkably; unforgettable
13. We've been going camping for years – mainly to the east coast – but this year we're off to Wales. ✓
14. a) solemn b) receipt c) castle d) island
15. The eagle <u>soared</u> from the clifftop, <u>swooping</u> down to <u>grab</u> its prey from the field below.
16.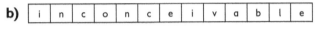
   in — active
   mis — understand
   il — literate
   dis — rational
   ir — continue
17. absorb**ent**; expect**ant**; excell**ent**; compli**ant**
18.

a)
s	h	i	e	l	d

b)
i	n	c	o	n	c	e	i	v	a	b	l	e

c)
p	i	e	c	e

d)
m	i	s	c	h	i	e	f

19. aisle – isle; bridal – bridle; morning – mourning; serial – cereal; profit – prophet; practise – practice
20. desert – dessert; proceed – precede; access – excess; addition – edition
21. **Answers will vary. Examples:**
   The **delicate** petals of the flowers had **started** to

   fragile — gradually — begun
   fade and were **slowly** falling to the ground.

Pages 88–97
Mixed questions
1. a) <u>The new library books</u> are on <u>the top shelf.</u>
   b) <u>Some helpful children</u> have tidied <u>the messy art area</u>.
   c) <u>The little kitten in the corner</u> is drinking <u>milk from a saucer</u>.
   d) <u>A roaring fire</u> warmed us from <u>the bitterly cold wind</u>.
2. a) We were driven to our destination by a reliable bus driver.
   b) The litter in the playground has been picked up by the children in Year 6.
   c) The statue was designed by a famous sculptor.
   d) My uncle was recommended for the job by his best friend.
3. a) Mum <u>has sewn</u> her ripped T-shirt.
   b) Some children in my class <u>have gone</u> on a school trip.
4. a) They have **eaten** their breakfast.
   b) Rory **saw** his friends last night.

5.

Sentence	Present perfect	Past perfect	Present progressive	Past progressive
Mark <u>has shown</u> great determination in overcoming his recent illness.	✓			
Sarena <u>is helping</u> Elise with her history homework.			✓	
I told Mum I <u>had tidied</u> my bedroom, but it wasn't true.		✓		
We <u>were watching</u> TV when you called.				✓

6. The fragile wings of the butterfly <u>caught</u> my immediate attention. I grabbed my camera, focused the lens and <u>captured</u> the beautiful creature as it landed on a flower.
7. The dog which you like best has won the best breed competition. ✓
8. a) Henry's been showing off again but as he's so funny we just laugh.
   b) If only you'd told me you were coming, I'd have made your favourite cake.
   c) It'll be rubbish if we can't go swimming at the weekend.
   d) I've had better test results since Mr Smith's been my teacher.
9. a) The cabin crew showed us to our seats.
   b) The cabin manager explained the safety procedures to us.
10. a) Martha is a gentle, **kind-hearted** girl who loves animals.
   b) Ethan, who is **fair-haired** with brown eyes, takes after his dad.
   c) Mum bought a **high-quality** sound system for the kitchen.
   d) Grandpa likes a **low-sugar** biscuit with his cup of tea.
11. obedi**ence**; confid**ence**; compli**ance**; signific**ance**
12. The vegetable competition at this year's village fair was won by Mr Hegarty. / At this year's village fair, the vegetable competition was won by Mr Hegarty.
13. Meg was <u>certain</u> she would commit to the holiday, despite a rather <u>dubious</u> report about the hotel.
14. After checking his **insurance** policy, Dad's **resistance** to claiming for the damage to his car vanished.
15.

Noun	Adjective	Noun	Adjective
caution	**cautious**	benefit	**beneficial**
nutrition	**nutritious**	torrent	**torrential**
grace	**gracious**	commerce	**commercial**
face	**facial**	suspect	**suspicious**

16. <u>It's</u> going to be raining all day so we are going to Huw's.

17. Tarek had seen the girls before: one was Mo's sister and the other was his cousin. ✓
18. believable; flexible; dependable; sensible
19. Dad was convinced he'd won the lottery – Mum wasn't so sure. ✓
20. a) I found Lilly's school bag behind the radiator in the cloakroom.
　　b) The sound of the horses' hooves as they neared the finish line was deafening.
　　c) The girls' hats are in the back of the car.
　　d) Parisa sewed a button on to Chris's / Chris' shirt.
21. On <u>the</u> farm, we saw <u>some</u> chickens, <u>lots of</u> cows and <u>two</u> horses. <u>The</u> farmer let me try milking <u>a</u> cow, which was good fun until I fell off <u>the</u> stool. It only had <u>three</u> legs so perhaps that is why.
22. Sean likes up-to-date fashion – he's a real trendsetter. ↑ ↑　　　　↑
　　　　　　　　　　　　　　　　H H 　　　D

23. a) Ivan worked <u>in</u> the garden all morning, then stopped <u>for</u> lunch.
　　b) I signed my name <u>at</u> the bottom <u>of</u> the page.
　　c) 'Have you ever been <u>to</u> my Gran's house <u>by</u> the sea?'

24.

Sentence	Relative pronoun	Coordinating conjunction	Subordinating conjunction
Unless you behave yourself, you are not going out to play.			✓
I always have butter and jam on my toast in the morning.		✓	
The leisure centre where I learnt to swim has shut down.	✓		

25. Has Craig always loved wild animals?
26. a) We visited our former neighbours <u>who moved to the coast last year</u>.
　　b) Last year, <u>when I had just turned seven</u>, Mum passed her driving test.
　　c) My dog Travis, <u>whose bark is very loud</u>, is actually a 'gentle giant'.
27. exclamation ✓
28. a) Elaya **had seen** the present under the tree and was sure it was hers!
　　b) The bird **had flown** from the nest to search for food for its chicks.
　　c) It was only after she **had left** the shop that Elise remembered her purse was still on the counter.
　　d) Mum **had forgotten** that it was her sister's birthday, so she raced out to buy a present.
29. My sick dog was examined by the caring vet. ✓
30. a) My <u>black</u> umbrella is very <u>scruffy</u>.
　　b) Will was <u>bored</u> with his <u>new</u> video game already.

　　c) <u>Choppy</u> seas and <u>gale-force</u> winds meant the boat could not set sail.
　　d) Lin-Lee decided her <u>new</u> shoes looked <u>odd</u>.
31. Eventually, they found the entrance to a hidden
　　　↑　　　　　　　　　　　↑　　　↑
　　　D　　　　　　　　　　　A　　 E　 C
　　cave and decided to explore it.
　　　　↑　　　　↑
　　　　B　　　　F

32. a) Maria put <u>some</u> glue on <u>the</u> back of <u>the</u> paper.
　　b) Please take <u>those</u> chocolate brownies out of <u>the</u> oven and cut them into <u>several</u> pieces.
33. **Answers will vary. Examples:**
　　My dog tried to **bite** my football.　　**verb**
　　I took a **bite** out of the apple.　　**noun**
34. **Answers will vary. Example:**
　　Christie trains **hard** so it is little wonder he is player of the match again.
35. a possessive pronoun ✓
36. At 7 o'clock sharp, the children and their parents arrived for parents' evening.
37. Dad likes to <u>garden</u> when he is off work. – **verb**
　　Dad likes to work in the <u>garden</u> when he is off work. – **noun**
38. a) A huge shark was found in <u>the shallow waters</u>.
　　b) Do you still have <u>that car</u> with the retractable roof?
　　c) Bertie dropped <u>her pencil</u> on the floor.
　　d) We waited for <u>the saline solution</u> to evaporate.
39. A mouse ran <u>across</u> the kitchen floor and <u>into</u> a hole <u>in</u> the wall.
40.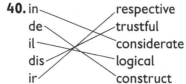
41. a) salmon　b) doubtful　c) thistle　d) lambing
42. The horses <u>raced</u> towards the finish line as the crowd <u>screamed</u> and <u>applauded</u>.
43. 'I'd like to introduce you to your new teacher,' said Mr McDermott.
44. Even though I'm not as fast as most of my friends, I love cross-country running.
45. Mum has lived in England a long time – twenty-five years to be exact – but she still misses her childhood home. **Also accept brackets or commas in place of the dashes.**

Glossary

abstract noun Names feelings, experiences or ideas that you cannot see or touch, e.g. love, courage.

active voice The subject of the sentence is carrying out the action – 'doing', 'being' or 'having'.

adjective Can be used before a noun, to modify it, or after the verb 'be', e.g. Sunni is tired.

adverb Can modify a verb, an adjective, another adverb or even a whole clause.

adverbial A word or phrase used like an adverb to modify a verb or clause. A **fronted adverbial** comes at the beginning of the sentence and is followed by a comma.

ambiguity Having more than one or meaning.

antonym A word opposite in meaning to another.

apostrophe Can be used in a contraction or to show possession.

brackets Punctuation marks that can be used to indicate a word or phrase in parenthesis.

bullet points Often used in non-fiction texts to show information, presenting it in an easy-to-read, list form.

clause A group of words that includes a subject and a verb.

collective noun Names a group of things or people, e.g. an **army** of ants.

colon Can be used after a clause, to introduce another clause that explains or gives more detail about the first; to introduce a quotation; and in play scripts after a character's name, to introduce their lines.

comma Used to separate items in a list. In most lists, there is no comma after the last list item and the word 'and'. Commas can also be used to make the meaning clear. Commas are used after fronted adverbials and subordinate clauses that come at the beginning of a sentence.

command Telling someone to do something. A command sentence uses a **command verb** (or imperative).

compound word Where two words are joined to make one longer word, e.g. playground.

contraction The shortened form of a word, where an apostrophe indicates an omitted letter or letters.

coordinating conjunction Words, phrases and clauses can be linked (coordinated) as an equal pair by the coordinating conjunctions *and, but* and *or*.

dash/dashes A single dash can be used at the start of a clause, adding additional information to the preceding clause. It can also be used for dramatic effect, to signal an interruption or a change in direction. A pair of dashes can be used to indicate a word or phrase in parenthesis.

determiner Introduces a noun. It tells us whether the noun is specific (known), e.g. **the** book, or non-specific (unknown), e.g. **a** book.

digraph Two letters that represent one sound, e.g 'ei'.

direct speech Reporting speech using the actual words said. Direct speech is shown using **speech marks**.

etymology The study of the origin of words and how they have changed over time.

exclamation sentence Starts with 'What...', or 'How...', contains a verb, and ends with an exclamation mark.

formal speech and writing Used in more 'serious' contexts such as delivering a speech or applying for a job.

homophone A word that sounds the same as another word but with a different meaning and spelling.

hyphen Can be used to join two words to make a compound word, to act as an adjective before a noun, and thus avoid ambiguity. Also used when a prefix ending in a vowel is added to a word starting with a vowel.

imperative A command verb, e.g. **Finish** your homework.

indirect speech Reporting speech without using speech marks, e.g. He said he would help me.

informal speech and writing A relaxed, 'chatty' way of communicating with family and friends, often using slang and contracted words.

inverted commas Sometimes called **speech marks**, come at the start and end of the spoken words. The closing inverted commas come *after* the final punctuation mark at the end of the direct speech.

main clause A clause that makes sense on its own.

mnemonic A way of helping you remember how to spell tricky words.

modal verbs Can be used to express degrees of certainty, ability, permission or obligation. They come before the main verb in a sentence.

near-homophone A word which sounds almost the same as another word but has a different spelling and meaning.

negative prefix A prefix added to the beginning of a word to make it negative, e.g. *un* in *unhappy*.

Non-Standard English Use of English that does not follow the rules of the Standard English dialect.

noun Naming words for people, places, animals and things.

noun phrase When you modify a noun with another word, e.g. a determiner and/or an adjective, it becomes a noun phrase. When more adjectives are added, it becomes an **expanded noun phrase**.

object The noun, proper noun, pronoun or noun phrase that is being 'acted upon' by the subject.

parenthesis A word or phrase inserted into a sentence as an explanation or an afterthought. The punctuation marks used to demarcate the parenthesis can be brackets, dashes or commas.

passive voice The noun, noun phrase or pronoun that would have been the object in the active voice becomes the subject, and 'receives' the action. It is formed by combining the verb 'to be' with the past participle of the verb.

past participle Formed by adding '-ed' to the root word, e.g. talk ➔ talk**ed**.

past perfect tense Can be used to show an action that was completed *before* another point in the past. It is formed by using the past tense of the verb 'to have' and the past participle of the verb.

past progressive tense   Shows a continuous action in the past. It is formed from the simple past tense of the verb 'to be' and the present participle of the main verb.

possession   Owning something, shown by the apostrophe, e.g. Henry's coat.

possessive determiner   Shows ownership of the following noun, e.g. My book, your book, his/her/its book, their book.

possessive pronoun   Shows ownership of a noun. It replaces the owner and the item that they own. e.g. It is mine.

prefix   A letter/letters added to the beginning of a word to make another word, e.g. regular/**ir**regular; heat/**re**heat.

preposition   Shows the relationship between a noun, proper noun or pronoun and other words in a sentence or clause. It can show position or location, direction or time. It can also introduce the object of a verb.

prepositional phrase   A phrase that contains a preposition, e.g. **under** the chair, **by** many people.

present participle   Formed by adding '-ing' to the basic form of the verb, e.g. eat ➔ eat**ing**.

present perfect tense   Shows an action or state that **has been** completed at some time in the past, e.g. He has been to London. It is formed by using the present tense of 'to have' and the past participle of the verb. It can also show an action or state which began in the past and continues to the present time, e.g. She **has taken** the dog for a walk.

present progressive tense   Shows an action that is continuing to happen. It is formed from the simple present tense of the verb 'to be' and the present participle of the main verb.

pronoun   Can replace a noun, proper noun or noun phrase.

proper noun   Can name a particular person or place. Starts with a capital letter.

question   A sentence that asks something. It starts with a capital letter and ends with a question mark.

question tag   A question can be in the form of a statement followed by a question tag, e.g. It's hot today, **isn't it?**

relative clause/relative pronoun   Gives more information about the preceding noun, noun phrase or proper noun. It is introduced by a relative pronoun. A relative clause is dependent on a main clause to make sense.

root word   The basic form of a word, before a suffix or prefix is added.

silent letters   Letters that are no longer sounded today, despite remaining in the words.

semi-colon   Can be used instead of a full stop to link two closely related independent clauses. It can also be used to separate items in a list where list items contain commas.

simple past tense   Used when we talk about an event or state of being or having that has already happened.

simple present tense   Used when we talk about an event or state of being that is happening now or that happens regularly.

Standard English   Using correct grammar.

statement   A sentence that tells you something. It starts with a capital letter and ends with a full stop.

stressed and unstressed syllables   A stressed syllable is one that is emphasised, e.g. *reference* – the first syllable, *ref*, is stressed, whereas the second two, *er* and *ence*, are unstressed.

subject   The person or thing that is carrying out the action, shown by the verb.

subjunctive form   Can be used in formal speech and writing, often in a subordinate clause, or to express a wish.

subordinating conjunction/subordinate clause   A subordinating conjunction (e.g. because, until) introduces a subordinate clause; a subordinate clause is dependent on a main clause, otherwise it doesn't make sense.

suffix   A letter or letters added to the end of a word, changing its meaning.

syllable   The beats of a word. They can be counted, e.g. *word* has one syllable. Syllables have at least one vowel and possibly one or more consonants.

synonym   A word with the same or similar meaning as another word.

verb   Tells you what someone or something in a sentence is doing, being or having.

Acknowledgements

The authors and publisher are grateful to the copyright holders for permission to use quoted materials and images.

All images are ©Shutterstock.com and ©HarperCollinsPublishers

Every effort has been made to trace copyright holders and obtain their permission for the use of copyright material. The authors and publisher will gladly receive information enabling them to rectify any error or omission in subsequent editions. All facts are correct at time of going to press.

Published by Collins
An imprint of HarperCollins*Publishers*
1 London Bridge Street
London SE1 9GF

HarperCollinsPublishers
Macken House, 39/40 Mayor Street Upper,
Dublin 1, D01 C9W8, Ireland

ISBN: 978-0-00-846960-3

10 9 8 7 6 5 4

©HarperCollins*Publishers* Ltd. 2021

All rights reserved. No part of this publication may be reproduced, stored in a retrieval system, or transmitted, in any form or by any means, electronic, mechanical, photocopying, recording or otherwise, without the prior permission of Collins.

Without limiting the exclusive rights of any author, contributor or the publisher, any unauthorised use of this publication to train generative artificial intelligence (AI) technologies is expressly prohibited. HarperCollins also exercise their rights under Article 4(3) of the Digital Single Market Directive 2019/790 and expressly reserve this publication from the text and data mining exception.

British Library Cataloguing in Publication Data.

A CIP record of this book is available from the British Library.

Author: Shelley Welsh
Publisher: Fiona McGlade
Project Editor: Katie Galloway
Cover Design: Kevin Robbins and Sarah Duxbury
Inside Concept Design: Ian Wrigley
Page Layout: Q2A Media
Production: Karen Nulty

FSC
www.fsc.org
MIX
Paper
FSC™ C007454

Progress charts

Use these charts to record your results in the four Progress Tests. Colour in the questions that you got right to help you identify any areas that you might need to study and practise again. (These areas are indicated in the 'See page...' row in the charts.)

Progress test 1

	Q1	Q2	Q3	Q4	Q5	Q6	Q7	Q8	Q9	Q10	Q11	Q12	Q13	Q14	Q15	Q16	Q17	Q18	TOTAL /67
See page...	6	6	8	10	4	4,6,8, 12,14	14	4, 8	6	12	8	12	10	4, 8	18	16	8	12	

Progress test 2

	Q1	Q2	Q3	Q4	Q5	Q6	Q7	Q8	Q9	Q10	Q11	Q12	Q13	Q14	Q15	Q16	Q17	Q18	TOTAL /51
See page...	34	26	6	36	28	14	10	30	12	36	38	38	28, 30	24	30	34, 36	34	24, 26	

Progress test 3

	Q1	Q2	Q3	Q4	Q5	Q6	Q7	Q8	Q9	Q10	Q11	Q12	Q13	Q14	Q15	Q16	Q17	Q18	Q19	Q20	Q21	TOTAL /55
See page...	46	28, 46	50	34	45	52	18	56	56	54	6	34, 36	58	56	50	14	56	48	50	56	16	

Progress test 4

	Q1	Q2	Q3	Q4	Q5	Q6	Q7	Q8	Q9	Q10	Q11	Q12	Q13	Q14	Q15	Q16	Q17	Q18	Q19	Q20	Q21	TOTAL /70
See page...	70	34	54	70	38	64	64	70	68	54	70	72	52	80	8	66	70	78	82	82	64	

Record your results here for the Mixed questions on pages 88–97

Mixed questions	Total score:	/ 138 marks